REGENTS RENAISSANCE DRAMA SERIES

General Editor: Cyrus Hoy
Advisory Editor: G. E. Bentley

THE FAIR MAID OF THE WEST

Parts I and II

THOMAS HEYWOOD

The Fair Maid of the West

PARTS I AND II

Edited by

ROBERT K. TURNER, JR.

UNIVERSITY OF NEBRASKA PRESS · LINCOLN

Regents Renaissance Drama Series

The purpose of the Regents Renaissance Drama Series is to provide soundly edited texts, in modern spelling, of the more significant plays of the Elizabethan, Jacobean, and Caroline theater. Each text in the series is based on a fresh collation of all sixteenth- and seventeenth-century editions. The textual notes, which appear above the line at the bottom of each page, record all substantive departures from the edition used as the copy-text. Variant substantive readings among sixteenth- and seventeenth-century editions are listed there as well. In cases where two or more of the old editions present widely divergent readings, a list of substantive variants in editions through the seventeenth century is given in an appendix. Editions after 1700 are referred to in the textual notes only when an emendation originating in some one of them is received into the text. Variants of accidentals (spelling, punctuation, capitalization) are not recorded in the notes. Contracted forms of characters' names are silently expanded in speech prefixes and stage directions, and, in the case of speech prefixes, are regularized. Additions to the stage directions of the copy-text are enclosed in brackets. Stage directions such as "within" or "aside" are enclosed in parentheses when they occur in the copy-text.

Spelling has been modernized along consciously conservative lines. "Murther" has become "murder," and "burthen," "burden," but within the limits of a modernized text, and with the following exceptions, the linguistic quality of the original has been carefully preserved. The variety of contracted forms (*'em, 'am, 'm, 'um, 'hem*) used in the drama of the period for the pronoun *them* are here regularly given as *'em*, and the alternation between *a'th'* and *o'th* (for *on* or *of the*) is regularly reproduced as *o'th'*. The copy-text distinction between preterite endings in *-d* and *-ed* is preserved except where the elision of *e* occurs in the penultimate syllable; in such cases, the final syllable is contracted. Thus, where the old editions read "threat'ned," those of the present series read "threaten'd." Where, in the old editions, a contracted preterite in *-y'd* would yield *-i'd* in modern spelling (as in "try'd," "cry'd," "deny'd"), the word is here given in its full form (e.g., "tried," "cried," "denied").

Punctuation has been brought into accord with modern practices. The effort here has been to achieve a balance between the generally light pointing of the old editions, and a system of punctuation which, without overloading the text with exclamation marks, semicolons, and dashes, will **make** the often loosely flowing verse (and prose) of the original syntactically intelligible to the modern reader. Dashes are regularly used only to indicate interrupted speeches, or shifts of address within a single speech.

Explanatory notes, chiefly concerned with glossing obsolete words and phrases, are printed below the textual notes at the bottom of each page. References to stage directions in the notes follow the admirable system of the Revels editions, whereby stage directions are keyed, decimally, to the line of the text before or after which they occur. Thus, a note on 0.2 has reference to the second line of the stage direction at the beginning of the scene in question. A note on 115.1 has reference to the first line of the stage direction following line 115 of the text of the relevant scene.

CYRUS HOY

University of Rochester

Contents

List of Abbreviations

Bates
"*A Woman Killed with Kindness*" and "*The Fair Maid of the West*," ed. Katherine Lee Bates. The Belles-Lettres Series. Boston, New York, and Chicago, 1917. (Part I only.)

Brereton
J. LeGay Brereton. "Notes on the Text of Thomas Heywood" in *Elizabethan Drama Notes and Studies*. Sydney, 1909.

Collier
The First and Second Parts of the Fair Maid of the West, ed. J. Payne Collier. London, 1850.

Dialogues
Thomas Heywood. *Pleasant Dialogues and Dramas*. London, 1637.

Dyce's notes
Manuscript notes in the copy of Q formerly owned by the Rev. Alexander Dyce and now in the Victoria and Albert Museum. Undated; assumed to be subsequent to Collier.

OED
The Oxford English Dictionary. 13 vols. Oxford, 1933.

Q
The first edition of Parts I and II, a quarto of 1631. In textual notes $Q(c)$ designates Q readings corrected by a proofreader, $Q(u)$ the uncorrected version of the same.

Shepherd
The Fair Maid of the West. Or, A Girl Worth Gold. The first part and *The second part*. In *The Dramatic Works of Thomas Heywood . . . in Six Volumes* [ed. R. H. Shepherd]. London, 1874. Vol. II.

S.D.
stage direction

S.P.
speech prefix

Tilley
M. P. Tilley. *A Dictionary of the Proverbs in England in the Sixteenth and Seventeenth Centuries*. Ann Arbor, 1950.

Verity
Thomas Heywood, ed. A. Wilson Verity. The Mermaid Series. London and New York, [1888]. (Part I only.)

Introduction

THE AUTHOR

In the notes to his *Specimens of English Dramatic Poets*, Charles Lamb, with a typical gentleness of temper, spoke of Thomas Heywood as "a sort of prose Shakspeare." However much (or little) the comparison tells us about Heywood's literary achievement, it is in another respect apt, for Heywood's and Shakespeare's careers were similar in a remarkable number of external particulars. Neither was a Londoner by birth, but at very nearly the same time both came to the city as young men to live by the theater. Both sought literary reputations in non-dramatic work, but both found their securest places in a three-fold relationship with the dramatic world, as actors, playwrights, and sharers in the management of theatrical companies. Both were professionals in the best sense of that term; they knew their art and were quietly proud of their ability to practice it, although Heywood, as far as we know, was less troubled than Shakespeare in this regard by aspirations to gentility. Shakespeare enjoyed the greater contemporary reputation, but Heywood lived longer and wrote more. If at last we must conclude that as a playwright Heywood was nowhere near Shakespeare's class, that hard judgment does not condemn him out of hand. Heywood appears to have known his limitations and rarely, if ever, to have strained beyond them; he may have been, as T. S. Eliot remarked, "a facile and sometimes felicitous purveyor of goods to the popular taste," but that "sometimes felicitous" deserves respect, covering, as it does, *The English Traveller* and *A Woman Killed with Kindness*.

Heywood was born about 1574 in Lincolnshire, probably a clergyman's son.[1] He seems to have spent perhaps two years at Cambridge (1591–1593) but to have left without a degree. His first substantial

[1] Arthur Melville Clark, *Thomas Heywood Playwright and Miscellanist* (1931) remains the standard biography. There is a convenient later summary of what is known of Heywood's life in Gerald Eades Bentley, *The Jacobean and Caroline Stage* (1956), IV, 553–557.

literary effort is likely to have been a narrative poem in the lushly Ovidian manner of Shakespeare's *Venus and Adonis* (*Oenone and Paris*, published in 1594 as by "T. H."), but by 1596 he was writing plays; in that year Philip Henslowe, owner of the Rose Theater and financial backer of several dramatic companies, recorded an advance of thirty shillings to the actors "for hawodes bocke."[2] Heywood may have begun as an actor and worked his way into doctoring the plays of others as well as writing entirely on his own account; certainly he was playing two years later when Henslowe received him as a "covenante searvante for ij yeares . . . not to playe any wher publicke a bowt london . . . but in my howsse."[3] It was in 1598 as well that in *Palladis Tamia* Francis Meres included Heywood in a rather indiscriminate heap of writers who were the "best for Comedy amongst us," together with Shakespeare and, among others, Rowley, Munday, Greene, Nash, and "Doctor Gager of Oxforde."

In the late 1590's Heywood's name appears frequently in Henslowe's records, but most of the plays for which he received payment have been lost.[4] The main line of his career, however, was established in these years. About the turn of the century he joined the Earl of Worcester's Men (Queen Anne's after 1603) as actor-writer and eventually became a sharer in the company. These players performed in public theaters—the Rose, the Curtain, and the Red Bull—which invited the patronage of the generality of playgoers; the plays they favored tended to be more romantic, more conservative morally, and less sophisticated intellectually and dramatically than those offered at such private houses as the Blackfriars. The milieu in which Heywood worked thus drew him to the sorts of drama that were the staple fare of the Jacobean stage, among them historical plays with interlacings of low comedy (the anonymous *If You Know Not Me*), bourgeois comedies and tragedies (*The Wise-Woman of Hogsden* and *A Woman Killed with Kindness*), plays on classical subjects which brought culture to the masses (the *Ages*), and melodramas of romantic adventure (*The Four Prentices of London*). His best known work was done in the first fifteen years of the seventeenth century, and if we are to believe his famous claim that *The English Traveller* (printed 1633) is but one play "reserved amongst two hundred and twenty, in which I have had either an entire hand, or at least a maine finger," he must have written

2 R. A. Foakes and R. T. Rickert, eds., *Henslowe's Diary* (1961), p. 50.

3 *Ibid.*, p. 241.

4 See Appendix C.

furiously. He seems, however, to have given no attention to the preservation of his dramatic writing. Some plays, including two collaborations, made their way to publishers and one, *The Captives*, survived in manuscript, but only sixteen were printed with his name on their title pages.[5]

None of the plays we have can reasonably be dated between 1614 and 1624.[6] Perhaps this apparent ten-year hiatus in Heywood's dramatic authorship was caused partially by his increasing involvement in a lengthy series of miscellaneous works (including occasional verse, translations, pamphlets describing wondrous or edifying events, and compilations of instructive matter) which began in 1608 with a translation of Sallust, although few if any of these compositions either can confidently be attributed to these years. About 1624, however, Heywood seems to have been drawn back to drama by Christopher Beeston, whose companies, the Lady Elizabeth's and Queen Henrietta's Men, mounted by 1634 a half-dozen Heywood plays and masques at Beeston's Phoenix theater and at court. In the mid-thirties Heywood seems also to have written with Richard Brome several plays for the King's Men, including *The Late Lancashire Witches*, and simultaneously he became the chief writer of Lord Mayors' pageants, composing seven between 1631 and 1639. Nor did advancing years impede his non-dramatic output. During the thirties some of his most extensive prose was published, and he appears to have continued to write voluminously until the day in August, 1641, when he stepped from his desk into his grave.

DATE AND SOURCES

Although they make use of many of the same characters and involve them in roughly similar situations, the two parts of *The Fair Maid* seem to have been separately conceived, but no one has as yet succeeded in fixing very precisely the date of the composition of either part. It was once thought that Part I could be placed at 1604 because Mullisheg,

[5] To these sixteen and *The Captives*, *Edward IV* and the two parts of *If You Know Not Me* are usually added, "although the evidence [for attribution] for the former at least is by no means unassailable. Faced with this situation, scholars have naturally revelled in attempts to fill the two hundred or so blank spaces in the canon from the anonymous plays of the period, though with a singular lack of agreement" (Arthur Brown, "An Edition of the Plays of Thomas Heywood," *Renaissance Papers* [1954], p. 71).

[6] Bentley, IV, 556.

who announced that he is "now at last establish'd in the throne" and reigns "King of Fez and great Morocco" (Pt. I, IV.iii.3–5), was held to be the Mulai Sheik who "was proclaimed King at Fez" in that year.[7] But Warner G. Rice subsequently pointed out not only that Mulai Sheik was a title which was applied to three sixteenth-century Moroccan rulers but also that other allusions create an atmosphere that is "distinctly Elizabethan."[8] These include the references to the Islands' Voyage and the late success at Cadiz which open Act I; the treatment accorded Essex, which suggests that nothing had yet occurred to impair his reputation; and Mullisheg's and Bess's conversation about Queen Elizabeth in terms indicating that she still lived (Pt. I, V.i.87–102). Moreover, even if Mullisheg was drawn from the Mulai Sheik crowned in 1604, Heywood's typically loose way of dealing with historical material (illustrated by his treatment of the character of Bashaw Joffer, who is based remotely on a Djafer, viceroy of Algiers in the 1580's) would have permitted Mullisheg's elevation to monarchy somewhat before his time, and Mulai Sheik was known by reputation in Europe before he became king.[9] The other details of plot and language so far investigated have yielded no firmer arguments for dating. It may seem, for example, that the Moroccan episodes of the play were introduced partly to take advantage of the curiosity aroused by the six-month residence in London during 1600 and 1601 of a Moorish ambassador and his entourage, yet Moors had been represented on the Elizabethan stage before 1600. Or one may notice that at I.ii.169–170 Forset asks Bess to meet Spencer "o'th' Hoe/ Near to the new-made fort." He is alluding to a structure upon which work began in the late 1580's and which was sufficiently completed by 1596 to have a garrison installed. "New-made," as opposed to simply "new," sounds close to the event; yet Forset is supposed to be speaking of things as they were in 1597, and presumably the Plymouth fort could have been generally referred to in some such terms (to distinguish it from the earlier Castle) until it was replaced by the Citadel

[7] Ross Jewell, "Thomas Heywood's *The Fair Maid of the West*" in *Studies in English Drama, First Series*, ed. Allison Gaw (1917), p. 67. Jewell reviews conjectures as to the date of Part I by earlier historians of the drama. Because of an apparent allusion to *The Fair Maid* in *The Roaring Girl* (pub. 1611) and the appearance in 1609 of a pamphlet on Muly-Sheck, A. M. Clark dated Part I in 1609–1610 (*op. cit.*, p. 110).

[8] Warner G. Rice, "The Moroccan Episode in Thomas Heywood's *The Fair Maid of the West*," *Philological Quarterly*, IX (1930), 134.

[9] *Ibid.*, pp. 135–137.

about 1670.[10] Some weight, however, must be given to the fact that all the apparent allusions now recognized are at least not inconsistent with a date somewhat earlier than 1604, and the consensus at present seems to agree with Collier's assertion that Part I was written "before the death of Elizabeth."[11]

Readers of Part II see in it differences from Part I "so great as to be accounted for only by an assumption of different authors or different periods of composition."[12] The circumstances of publication clearly establish the play as Heywood's, but no means has yet been found to determine its exact date either. Clark thought Part II "may have been written as a sequel to the first in consequence of the court performance" referred to in Heywood's prologue and epilogue,[13] but if the prologue and epilogue bracket both parts, as their placement in the first edition indicates, rather than the first only, as Clark believed, his suggestion cannot stand. Bentley disposes of the few other pieces of evidence which have been adduced and settles on a date of about 1630 as implied by the history of the company which performed the play and the careers of the actors named in the dramatis personae included in the first edition.[14] If Heywood drew any details of the Florentine episode of Part II, such as the conflict between Ferrara and Mantua or the name of Florence's commander at sea, Petro Deventuro, from a specific source, it has not been discovered. What slight evidence there is, then, indicates that Heywood wrote Part II some twenty-five or thirty years after Part I.

Heywood does not, in fact, seem to have based any of the components of the play on a specific source, but there is nothing particularly original in his characters or in the incidents of his plot. Bess, as she herself points out (Pt. I, II.iii.13), is kin to ballad and chapbook heroines who, though lower-class, are ennobled by modesty and

[10] The story of the Moorish embassy is told by Bernard Harris, "A Portrait of a Moor," *Shakespeare Survey XI* (1958), pp. 89–97. For Plymouth fortifications, see R. N. Worth, *History of Plymouth* (1890), pp. 402–428 *et passim.*

[11] J. Payne Collier, *A History of English Dramatic Poetry* (1831), I, 403, where the statement applies to both parts, but this is corrected on p. xxii. Bentley officially dates Part I before 1610, but adds that he is "inclined towards a date before 1603" (IV, 568). Rice believes Part I was "framed before the turn of the century" (p. 137).

[12] Bentley, IV, 568.

[13] *Op. cit.*, p. 110.

[14] Bentley, IV, 571.

virtuous love and who, when the occasion required, disguised themselves as men to engage in high adventure. An Elizabethan pamphlet,
The Life and Pranks of Long Meg of Westminster (1590), could easily have
supplied Bess's initial outline ("the occupation of inn-keeping, the
gaining of wealth that was freely bestowed in charity, the incident of
the duel in which Roughman is discomfited, the love of fun, the firm
rule over servants and customers, and the submissive devotion to the
man of her choice"[15]), and if Heywood failed to notice the pamphlet,
he is certain to have known a play on Long Meg now lost but acted
by the Admiral's Men, Henslowe's company, from 1595. Spencer, the
gallant and honorable lover; Goodlack, the faithful friend; Roughman, the reformed coward; Clem, the shrewdly stupid clown;
Florence, the high-minded but passionate Italian prince—all have
numerous antecedents in drama or non-dramatic romance. Even
Moorish Mullisheg and Joffer, the most exotic of the characters, had
appeared under different names earlier than Part I in such plays as
Peele's *Battle of Alcazar* (1588–1589) and the anonymous *Captain
Thomas Stukeley* (1596) and were by the time of Part II to have become
familiar figures on the stage, as was the type to which Tota belongs.[16]
The incidents of the plot were equally conventional. Whatever elements of Bess's and Spencer's careers were not present in the story of
Long Meg could have been suggested by the motif of separated lovers
present in a number of ballads (some of which include a love-test
similar to Goodlack's onslaught upon Bess's fidelity to Spencer in Pt. I,
III.iii–iv) as well as by analogous tales told in a half-dozen Italian
novelle, including Cinthio's story "Of Fineo and Fiamma" which
appeared in English in *Riche his Farewell to Militarie Profession* (1581).[17]
Borrowings of character, plot, and even techniques of rendering
material were not unusual in Elizabethan drama, which constantly
made new mixtures of old ingredients. If *The Fair Maid* seems more
dependent than many other plays on stock romantic elements, that
impression may direct us to an important characteristic of the kind of
drama it is, a kind in which conventionality, up to a point, is a virtue.

---

[15] Katherine Lee Bates, ed., "*A Woman Killed with Kindness*" and "*The
Fair Maid of the West*" (1917), p. 141. See also Louis B. Wright, *Middle Class
Culture in Elizabethan England* (1958), p. 411.

[16] See Eldred Jones, *Othello's Countrymen* (1965), especially pp. 109–116
and Appendix I.

[17] See Warren E. Roberts, "Ballad Themes in *The Fair Maid of the West*,"
Journal of American Folklore, LXVIII (1955), 19–23, and Rice, pp. 137–140.

THE PLAY

Adventure drama is always with us even though it gets low critical marks for being a fundamentally unserious form of art. Instead of asking us better to understand ourselves and our world by seeing through experience, it invites us to reject reality as commonplace and deep concerns as troublesome, and temporarily to substitute for them a fantastic world of simple, straightforward emotions, black and white morality, absolute poetic justice, and, above all, violent rapidity of action. If boredom is the perennial disability of men, adventure stories are the perennial therapy, operating as a restorative by encouraging an intermission in the ordinary powers and interests of the mind. Nearly all great fictions are fundamentally adventures, but while they use incident to open matters of philosophical concern, adventure drama proper uses incident to cancel such matters, to replace subtlety with simplicity, and to obliterate grey with vivid primary colors, often blood red. Instead of reaching for a metaphysical or psychological fourth dimension, adventure drama deals in length and breadth only; and its success is in part measured by the degree to which swiftness of movement prevents any significant meaning from arising. If this be fraud, men have been happy to make the most of it, at least occasionally.

The Fair Maid has features typical of Elizabethan bourgeois literature, but its primary relationship is with all adventure narratives regardless of their era. The opening scenes of Part I are designed to effect a transition from everyday surroundings to the world of high events. The Cadiz raid and the Islands' Voyage were affairs which were invested by Elizabethans with a spirit of heroism in excess of their actual achievement; they were real, but they were the stuff of fiction.[18] If on the eve of the Islands' Voyage the streets of Plymouth glistered with English gold and gallantry, dashing gentlemen with honor on their minds, money in their purses and, for the moment, time on their hands, it is only appropriate that the actual town contain at least one girl worthy of them, beautiful enough, affable enough, and honorable (which is to say, chaste) enough. So we meet Bess Bridges, whose invincible virtue may be superhuman, but who, like ordinary you and me, has a real job (as a barmaid) in a real place (the Castle) and a real biography (sent to service by her trade-fallen father, a seller of hides in Somersetshire). And when lusty and brave gallants drink

[18] See Appendix A.

wine, fights do occur; Carrol is killed and we are projected into a series of events which seem naturally consequent but which are increasingly the fantastic matter of the adventure genre. Heywood has, in fact, so outmaneuvered our critical sense, that he can soon have his way with us altogether. Is it very likely that at Fayal Spencer should be wounded in a duel in which another Spencer is killed? Even with fidelity given as her strong suit, would Bess turn down Goodlack, Roughman, and the mayor's son of Foy, dispose of her prosperous tavern, and take to the high seas in disguise only to bring home a dead lover? Unless we are in an unreasonably ugly mood, we have forgotten to ask the questions by the time the events are sprung upon us, and it is in this connection that conventionality becomes a dramatic asset. Shock and surprise set the mind to work; the recognition of old acquaintances sets it at ease. Thus the characters are stock figures, and they very frequently do or say stock things. The dialogue is littered with proverbs. Clem parodies lines from *The Spanish Tragedy*, a dramatic joke we all know and always smile at. Spencer has a Stoical speech on the vagaries of fortune (Pt. I, II.ii.5–13); he is far from being a Stoical character, but we know he is simply saying what all good men do when they have been mishandled by adversity. Bess plays straight man to Clem in a piece of stand-up comedy as old in its technique as Dionysus. We are secure among such familiar articles of dramatic furniture, so secure that the preposterous can slip by us in disguise.

Speed and timing of incident keep disbelief suspended, and to allow for the necessary variety *The Fair Maid* is put together in the simplest possible way. Once the exposition is established and the plot set in motion by Carrol's death, Heywood attaches episode to episode until he has a play's worth, whereupon he allows virtue to triumph over infatuation in Mullisheg in order to achieve the finality of a marriage of the principals. There is no more inevitability in Mullisheg's declaration for honor than there is in his contrary declaration for lust that opens Part II, except that all the world knows about the caprice of barbaric kings. Episodic structure, however, not only permits variety of incident but also variety of mood and effect. The comic discomfiture of Roughman can be set against the pathos of Bess's trial by Goodlack; Spencer's elevating defiance of his Spanish captors can be followed by a bit of low horseplay on Clem's part and this by the galloping sentimentality of Bess's last will and testament in favor of the poor folk of Foy; the exhibition of Mullisheg's royal lechery as he plans to stock his Alkedavy with an international sorority of concubines is only moments away from the purity of Bess's resolution to erect a lasting monument over the remains of her beloved Spencer. English virtue and courage, if we ever had any doubt of them, shine out over Fezzian vice and Spanish pusillanimity; and such emotions as national pride become just as much subject to Heywood's manipulation as the pleasurable disappointment aroused in Pt. I, IV.iv when Bess and Spencer do not quite recognize one another because Goodlack is conveniently out of the way nursing a flesh wound.

Not only disbelief but the audience's sense of the ridiculous has to be held in abeyance during such scenes. In addition, the writer of adventure drama has another enemy to deal with, particularly if his audience is oriented toward a Puritanical ethic of all work and no play. Because there is something immoral about one's enjoying himself at the expense of reality, the dramatist must provide compensation, and this Heywood does by incorporating, particularly into Part I, great slices of bourgeois morality. We need not feel guilty about participating in Bess's adventures when she and her companions are so clearly on the right side, such paragons of thrift and benevolence, such respecters of law and order, such models of the decent Protestant virtues. To object to a fiction so explicitly exhibiting these qualities is virtually to object to a sermon. And combined with Spencer's and Bess's altruism is an admirable providence; their ideals do not forbid their accepting the fortune pressed on them by Mullisheg, for there is no sensible reason why virtue should not be rewarded in hard cash.

Although many of the devices of Part I carry over to Part II just as do the major characters, every critic of *The Fair Maid* has recognized pronounced differences in the moral tone of the two parts. The action of Part II begins with the same mechanism of character reversal which furnished an impetus for the second part of Dekker's *Honest Whore* (1604–1605); Mullisheg, who at the end of Part I had suppressed his rather bewildered infatuation with Bess, now burns with a lust which has a counterpart in Tota's Italianate jealousy and desire for revenge. So many bed-tricks had been successfully executed by 1630 that one wonders why Goodlack had such difficulty in thinking of this device as a solution to the heroes' problems, but the very fact that he did has a bearing on the moral tone of the play. However familiar the device may have been, it seems nevertheless to have carried with it a certain moral ambiguity, although in this instance Heywood plays safe by doubling the number of dupes and having them married to one another rather than merely betrothed.[19] Through these means the atmosphere of Part II becomes viciously charged, and when Spencer and Joffer enter into a contract which requires personal honor to override all other considerations, we are in a world of Fletcherian absolutes that obviously has different moral bases from that of Part I. The same tone is present in the Florentine episode of Part II. In Part I Bess's beauty and goodness were twin shields against evil; Goodlack could no more force himself upon her than a lion can attack a virgin. In Part II, however, her beauty becomes a stimulus to rape, and when she is saved from the Captain of the Banditti by Florence's happy intervention, she is delivered to a man who though more polite is only slightly less aggressive. The exaggerated love-honor conflict in which Spencer is subsequently caught up and the deception wrought upon us when Bess declares her desire to be revenged on Spencer (Pt. II, V.ii.78–82) but actually works to effect their escape from another difficult situation are sorts of material dearer to Jacobean than to Elizabethan hearts. Whether Heywood chose to deal with such melodramatic themes because they were fashionable or because he was writing for an aristocratic rather than a popular audience, their effect is to make Part II a less innocent and a less vigorously healthy play than Part I.

THE TEXT

Parts I and II were issued together when the play was first published. Both were entered in the Stationers' Register to Richard Royston on June 16, 1631; the quarto which appeared pursuant to this entry was printed anonymously for Royston. It has the appearance of two separate books, each with its own title page and preliminaries and its own signature alphabet (Part I collates A–I⁴; Part II A–L⁴ M²). Part I is paged but Part II is not. There are many indications, nevertheless, that the two parts were printed as one book, the most conspicuous being that the two title pages were clearly impressed from the same setting, the only difference between them being a change from "The first part" to "The second part" or vice versa. In the early 1630's Royston had several books printed by Miles Flesher;

[19] A discussion of the moral significance of the bed-trick may be found in Clifford Leech, "The Theme of Ambition in *All's Well that Ends Well*," *A Journal of English Literary History*, XXI (1954), 25–26.

The Fair Maid as well seems to have been a product of Flesher's house. It evidently was set by one compositor in a rather complicated way, sometimes *seriatim* and sometimes by formes, which apparently was adopted because of some requirement of the management of the work in the shop (perhaps because another book was being printed concurrently) rather than because of difficulties in the copy. As far as one can tell, the text was accurately reproduced.[20]

Although the presence of the dedicatory epistles and addresses to the reader before both parts makes it clear that the publisher and Heywood were in touch at the time the quarto was printed, there is nothing to show that Heywood provided the text or even reviewed it. From the manuscripts of *The Captives* and *The Escapes of Jupiter*, we know that Heywood wrote a difficult hand; the small number of misreading errors, or substantive errors of any sort, in the quarto of *The Fair Maid* therefore points away from a Heywood autograph immediately underlying the print. Moreover, the quarto is generally lacking in stage directions or other features which we recognize as technically theatrical.

The title pages of both parts proclaim that the printed version of *The Fair Maid* is being presented "As it was lately acted before the King and Queen, with approved liking." The prologue and epilogue were written to be "spoken to their two Majesties at Hampton Court," as Heywood tells us when he included them, with revisions, in *Pleasant Dialogues and Dramas* (1637), and Professor Bentley suggests that the actor lists included in the quarto reflect the composition of Queen Henrietta's Men in 1630 or 1631 and notes that this company gave three performances at Hampton Court between October 10, 1630, and February 20, 1630/31.[21] Preceding a court performance, one supposes that a dramatic company might have to furnish a transcript of the play for official review, and it is not unlikely that a scribal copy of both parts of *The Fair Maid* would have been made for this purpose and afterwards been available for printer's copy. In any case, the uniformity of spelling, punctuation, and other accidentals, the

[20] A collation of eight copies of Part I and ten of Part II turned up no press-variants of any significance. A complete report of these and a more extensive discussion of the bibliographical features of the book may be found in "The Text of Heywood's *The Fair Maid of the West*," *The Library*, 5th series, forthcoming.

[21] IV, 570.

occasionally unsuccessful struggles with Heywood's verse lineation (about thirty instances in Part I and forty in Part II), the evident legibility of the copy, and slight signs of sophistication in both parts[22] suggest that some sort of scribal transcript of Heywood's papers was sold by the company to Royston. The text, the prologue, the epilogue, and the actor lists seem to have been part of this manuscript; only the epistles to Othow and Hammon and those to the reader must have come to the printer directly from Heywood.

If this supposition is right, we probably have in the Q text a rather sophisticated version of what Heywood wrote. Aside from a few obvious emendations, which have only the slightest effect on meaning, we can, however, get no closer than Q to the substance of Heywood's manuscript, and we must take it on faith that the scribe reproduced what he found in his copy, or if he made changes, that Heywood would not have objected. The accidentals are a somewhat different matter. The light system of punctuation of this edition is probably closer to Heywood's own usage (as represented in the manuscript of *The Captives*) than the generally heavy punctuation of Q. The lineation of Q, especially in Part IÌ, is sometimes dubious; and it has been silently altered (frequently after the example of earlier editions) where correction seemed either necessary or strongly desirable. In less compelling instances the Q lining has been retained. Again, the scribe is our only witness to Heywood's own preference in this matter, and we should give him the benefit of any doubts.

ROBERT K. TURNER, JR.

University of Wisconsin–Milwaukee

22 I take it that at Pt. I, III.ii.28 Heywood wrote "queen's lieutenant" and that this was updated to "king's lieutenant" by the scribe. I also find it peculiar that at Pt. II, IV.v.29 a character designated "Drawer" in stage direction and speech prefix announces, "Gentlemen, I draw none myself. . . ."

THE FAIR MAID OF THE WEST

Part I

To the Much Worthy and My Most Respected John Othow,
Esquire, Counsellor at Law, in the Noble Society of Gray's Inn

Sir,

    Excuse this my boldness (I entreat you) and let it pass
under the title of my love and respect long devoted unto you,
of which, if I endeavor to present the world with a due
acknowledgment without the sordid expectation of reward   5
or servile imputation of flattery, I hope it will be the rather
accepted. I must ingenuously acknowledge a weightier argument would have better suited with your grave employment,
but there are retirements necessarily belonging to all the
labors of the body and brain. If in any such cessation you will   10
deign to cast an eye upon this weak and unpolish'd poem, I
shall receive it as a courtesy from you much exceeding any
merit in me (my good meaning only accepted). Thus wishing
you healthful ability in body, untroubled content in mind,
with the happy fruition of both the temporal felicities of the   15
world present and the eternal blessedness of the life future,
I still remain as ever,

                    Yours, most affectionately devoted,
                        Thomas Heywood

    0.1. *John Othow*] Othow (Athow, Athowe) was born in 1592 and died in
1638. Once a fellow of Caius College, he became a barrister-at-law in
Gray's Inn in 1614 and an ancient (a member of the governing body) in
1627 (J. Venn and J. A. Venn, *Alumni Cantabrigiensis*, and Reginald J.
Fletcher, *The Pension-Book of Gray's Inn* [1569–1669]). Apart from the friendship to which this dedication and that to Part II testify, nothing is known of
his relationship with Heywood.
    7. *ingenuously*] frankly.
    7–8. *argument*] subject.
    11–13. *I shall . . . accepted*] possibly "I will receive your looking at my
poem as a courtesy exceeding my merit, granted only because you have
been kind enough to accept good intentions instead of merit" or, since *accept*
and *except* were more-or-less interchangeable, ". . . exceeding my merit,
which is slight except for my good meaning."

–3–

To the Reader

Courteous Reader, my plays have not been exposed to the
public view of the world in numerous sheets and a large
volume, but singly (as thou seest) with great modesty and
small noise. These comedies, bearing the title of *The Fair
Maid of the West*, if they prove but as gracious in thy private   5
reading as they were plausible in the public acting, I shall
not much doubt of their success. Nor need they (I hope)
much fear a rugged and censorious brow from thee, on whom
the greatest and best in the kingdom have vouchsafed to
smile. I hold it no necessity to trouble thee with the argu-   10
ment of the story, the matter itself lying so plainly before
thee in acts and scenes, without any deviations or winding
indents.

> *Peruse it through, and thou may'st find in it*
> *Some mirth, some matter, and perhaps some wit.*   15

He that would study thy content,
T. H.

---

6. *plausible*] favorably received, applauded.

13. *indents*] recesses (i.e., the story is straightforwardly told).

15. *Some . . . wit.*] Heywood liked this line well enough to use it again to
conclude the Prologue to *The English Traveller*.

PROLOGUE

[Spoken at Court]

Amongst the Grecians there were annual feasts
To which none were invited as chief guests
Save princes and their wives. Amongst the men
No argument could be disputed then
But who best govern'd, and (as't did appear)   5
He was proclaim'd sole sovereign for that year.
    The queens and ladies argued at that time
For beauty and for virtue who was prime,
And she had the like honor. Two here be,
For beauty one, the other majesty,   10
Most worthy (did that custom still persever)
Not for one year, but to be sovereigns ever.

4. No . . . be] *Dialogues; There was no argument Q.*
6. proclaim'd] *Dialogues; esteem'd Q.*
8. beauty . . . who] *Dialogues; Vertue and for beauty which Q.*
9. like] *Dialogues; high Q.*

5. *as't . . . appear*] in accordance with the resolution of the argument.

DRAMATIS PERSONAE

TWO SEA CAPTAINS
MR. CARROL, *a gentleman*
MR. SPENCER, by Mr. Michael Bowyer
CAPTAIN GOODLACK, *Spencer's friend*, by Mr. Richard Perkins
TWO VINTNER'S BOYS   5
BESS BRIDGES, *the Fair Maid of the West*, by Hugh Clark
MR. FORSET, *a gentleman*, by Christopher Goad
MR. ROUGHMAN, *a swaggering gentleman*, by William Shearlock
CLEM, *a drawer of wine under Bess Bridges*, by Mr. William Robinson
THREE SAILORS   10
A SURGEON
A KITCHENMAID, by Mr. Anthony Turner
THE MAYOR OF FOY
AN ALDERMAN *and a* SERVANT
A SPANISH CAPTAIN, by Christopher Goad   15
AN ENGLISH MERCHANT, by Robert Axell
MULLISHEG, *King of Fez*, by Mr. William Allen
BASHAW ALCADE, by Mr. [William] Wilbraham
BASHAW JOFFER
TWO SPANISH CAPTAINS   20
A FRENCH MERCHANT
AN ITALIAN MERCHANT
[A PREACHER]
A CHORUS
[SPANISH AND ENGLISH SAILORS, MOORS]   25

THE EARL OF ESSEX, *going to Cales*   ⎫
THE MAYOR OF PLYMOUTH *with* PETITIONERS   ⎬ *Mutes personated*
[CAPTAINS]   ⎭

12. Turner] $Q(c)$; Furner $Q(u)$.

0.1. *Dramatis Personae*] See Appendix B.

2. *Carrol*] Q spells *Caroll* here; *Caroll* and *Carrol* appear in the text.

8. *Roughman*] Q spells *Ruffman* here but *Roughman* subsequently in Part I.

20. *Two Spanish Captains*] the two Spaniards brought on at Pt. I, IV.iv.26.1.

26. *Cales*] Cadiz. The Earl, however, is going to the Azores, not to Cadiz.
Cf. Part I, I.i.1–7.

27. *Mutes personated*] non-speaking characters represented.

The Fair Maid of the West

or

A Girl Worth Gold

PART I

[I.i]   *Enter two* Captains *and* Mr. Carrol.

1 CAPTAIN.
    When puts my lord to sea?
2 CAPTAIN.   When the wind's fair.
CARROL.
    Resolve me, I entreat; can you not guess
    The purpose of this voyage?
1 CAPTAIN.   Most men think
    The fleet's bound for the Islands.
CARROL.   Nay, 'tis like.
    The great success at Cales under the conduct   5
    Of such a noble general hath put heart
    Into the English; they are all on fire
    To purchase from the Spaniard. If their carracks
    Come deeply laden, we shall tug with them
    For golden spoil.
2 CAPTAIN.   Oh, were it come to that!   10
1 CAPTAIN.
    How Plymouth swells with gallants! How the streets
    Glister with gold! You cannot meet a man
    But trick'd in scarf and feather, that it seems
    As if the pride of England's gallantry
    Were harbor'd here. It doth appear, methinks,   15

---

1. *my lord*] i.e., Robert Devereux, second Earl of Essex.
4. *Islands*] the Azores.   8. *purchase*] win, gain by conquest.
8. *carracks*] large ships, galleons.

A very court of soldiers.

CARROL.   It doth so.
   Where shall we dine today?
2 CAPTAIN.
   At the next tavern by; there's the best wine.
1 CAPTAIN.
   And the best wench, Bess Bridges, she's the flower
   Of Plymouth held. The Castle needs no bush;   20
   Her beauty draws to them more gallant customers
   Than all the signs i'th' town else.
2 CAPTAIN.   A sweet lass,
   If I have any judgment.
1 CAPTAIN.   Now, in troth,
   I think she's honest.
CARROL.   Honest, and live there?
   What, in a public tavern, where's such confluence   25
   Of lusty and brave gallants? Honest, said you?
2 CAPTAIN.
   I vow she is, for me.
1 CAPTAIN.   For all, I think.
   I'm sure she's wondrous modest.
CARROL.   But withal
   Exceeding affable.
2 CAPTAIN.   An argument
   That she's not proud.
CARROL.   No; were she proud, she'd fall.   30
1 CAPTAIN.
   Well, she's a most attractive adamant;
   Her very beauty hath upheld that house
   And gain'd her master much.
CARROL.   That adamant
   Shall for this time draw me too; we'll dine there.
2 CAPTAIN.
   No better motion. Come to the Castle then.   [Exeunt.]   35

34. too] Collier; to Q.

_____

   20. bush] tavern-sign (a bunch of ivy or other evergreen displayed to
advertise the tavern).
   24. honest] chaste.   26. brave] handsomely dressed.
   27. for me] as far as I am concerned.
   31. adamant] magnet.   35. motion] proposal.

[I.ii]   *Enter* Mr. Spencer *and* Captain Goodlack.

GOODLACK.
    What, to the old house still?
SPENCER.   Canst blame me, Captain?
    Believe me, I was never surpris'd till now,
    Or catch'd upon the sudden.
GOODLACK.   Pray resolve me,
    Why, being a gentleman of fortunes, means,
    And well revenu'd, will you adventure thus   5
    A doubtful voyage, when only such as I,
    Born to no other fortunes than my sword,
    Should seek abroad for pillage?
SPENCER.   Pillage, Captain?
    No, 'tis for honor; and the brave society
    Of all these shining gallants that attend   10
    The great lord general drew me hither first,
    No hope of gain or spoil.
GOODLACK.
    Ay, but what draws you to this house so oft?
SPENCER.
    As if thou knew'st it not.
GOODLACK.   What, Bess?
SPENCER.   Even she.
GOODLACK.
    Come, I must tell you, you forget yourself.   15
    One of your birth and breeding thus to dote
    Upon a tanner's daughter! Why, her father
    Sold hides in Somersetshire and being trade-fall'n
    Sent her to service.
SPENCER.   Prithee speak no more;
    Thou tell'st me that which I would fain forget   20
    Or wish I had not known. If thou wilt humor me,
    Tell me she's fair and honest.
GOODLACK.   Yes, and loves you.
SPENCER.
    To forget that were to exclude the rest;

---

1. *still*] once again, constantly.
2. *surpris'd*] taken by surprise.
18. *trade-fall'n*] bankrupt.

All saving that were nothing. Come, let's enter.

Enter two Drawers.

1 DRAWER

You are welcome, gentlemen. —Show them into the next   25
room there.

2 DRAWER.

Look out a towel and some rolls, a salt and trenchers.

SPENCER.

No, sir, we will not dine.

2 DRAWER.

I am sure ye would if ye had my stomach. What wine drink
ye, sack or claret?   30

SPENCER.

Where's Bess?

2 DRAWER.

Marry, above, with three or four gentlemen.

SPENCER.

Go call her.

2 DRAWER.

I'll draw you a cup of the neatest wine in Plymouth.

SPENCER.

I'll taste none of your drawing. Go call Bess.   35

2 DRAWER.

There's nothing in the mouths of these gallants but "Bess,
Bess."

SPENCER.

What sa'y, sir?

2 DRAWER.

Nothing, sir, but I'll go call her presently.

SPENCER

Tell her who's here.   40

---

27. *Look out*] select (and then fetch).
27. *towel*] tablecloth.
27. *trenchers*] plates.
29. *stomach*] appetite.
30. *sack*] white wine, usually Spanish.
30. *claret*] red wine, usually from Bordeaux.
34. *neatest*] purest, least watered.
38. *sa'y*] say ye.

2 DRAWER.

The devil rid her out of the house, for me.

SPENCER.

Sa'y, sir?

2 DRAWER.

Nothing but "Anon, anon," sir.

Enter Bess Bridges.

SPENCER.

See, she's come.

BESS.

Sweet Mr. Spencer, y'are a stranger grown.   45
Where have you been these three days?

SPENCER.   The last night
I sat up late at game. Here, take this bag
And lay't up till I call for't.

BESS.   Sir, I shall.

SPENCER.

Bring me some wine.

BESS.   I know your taste, and I
Shall please your palate.   [*Exit*.]

GOODLACK.   Troth, 'tis a pretty soul.   50

SPENCER.

To thee I will unbosom all my thoughts.
Were her low birth but equal with her beauty, More hot than poor
Here would I fix my love.

GOODLACK.   You are not mad, sir?
You say you love her?

SPENCER.   Never question that.

GOODLACK.

Then put her to't; win opportunity,   55
She's the best bawd. If, as you say, she loves you,
She can deny you nothing.

SPENCER.   I have proved her
Unto the utmost test, examin'd her
Even to a modest force, but all in vain.
She'll laugh, confer, keep company, discourse,   60
And something more, kiss; but beyond that compass

53. love] *this edn.*; thoughts *Q.*

She no way can be drawn.

GOODLACK.   'Tis a virtue
But seldom found in taverns.

Enter Bess *with wine.*

BESS.

'Tis of the best Graves wine, sir.

SPENCER.

Gramercy, girl; come sit.   65

BESS.

Pray pardon, sir, I dare not.

SPENCER.

I'll ha' it so.

BESS.

My fellows love me not and will complain
Of such a saucy boldness.

SPENCER.   Pox on your fellows!
I'll try whether their pottle pots or heads   70
Be harder if I do but hear them grumble.
Sit. Now, Bess, drink to me.

BESS.   To your good voyage!

Enter the Second Drawer.

2 DRAWER.

Did you call, sir?

SPENCER.
Yes, sir, to have your absence. Captain, this health.

GOODLACK.

Let it come, sir.   75

2 DRAWER.

Must you be set and we wait, with a ——

SPENCER.

What say you, sir?

2 DRAWER.

Anon, anon; I come there.   *Exit.*

SPENCER.

What will you venture, Bess, to sea with me?

---

64. *Graves wine*] from the Graves district, near Bordeaux.
70. *pottle pots*] half-gallon tankards.

BESS.

    What I love best, my heart, for I could wish   *gay*   80
    I had been born to equal you in fortune
    Or you so low to have been rank'd with me;
    I could have then presum'd boldly to say
    I love none but my Spencer.

SPENCER.   Bess, I thank thee.

    Keep still that hundred pound till my return   85
    From th'Islands with my lord. If never, wench,
    Take it; it is thine own.

BESS.   You bind me to you.

Enter the First Drawer.

1 DRAWER.

    Bess, you must fill some wine into the Portcullis; the gentle-
    men there will drink none but of your drawing.

SPENCER.

    She shall not rise, sir. Go, let your master snick-up.   90

1 DRAWER.

    And that should be cousin-german to the hick-up.   [*Exit.*]

Enter the Second Drawer.

2 DRAWER.

    Bess, you must needs come. The gentlemen fling pots, pottles,
    drawers, and all downstairs. The whole house is in an
    uproar.

BESS.

    Pray pardon, sir, I needs must be gone.   95

2 DRAWER.

    The gentlemen swear if she come not up to them, they will   *oh no*
    come down to her.

SPENCER.

    If they come in peace,
    Like civil gentlemen, they may be welcome;
    If otherwise, let them usurp their pleasures.   100

---

    88. *Portcullis*] the name of a room in the tavern, like the Mermaid
(II.i.51), the Crown (III.iii.105), and the Half-moon (IV.ii.96).
    90. *snick-up*] hang himself.
    91. *cousin-german*] first cousin (i.e., close kin: *snik-up* means "hiccup" in
Low German and *snik* means "gasp, sob" in Dutch [*OED*]).

We stand prepar'd for both.   [*Exit* Second Drawer.]

Enter Carrol *and two* Captains.

CARROL.

　　Save you, gallants. We are somewhat bold to press
　　Into your company. It may be held scarce manners,
　　Therefore fit that we should crave your pardon.

SPENCER.

　　Sir, you are welcome; so are your friends.   105

1 CAPTAIN.

　　Some wine!

BESS.

　　Pray give me leave to fill it.

SPENCER.

　　You shall not stir. —So please you, we'll join company.—
　　Drawer, more stools!

CARROL.

　　I take't that's a she-drawer. —Are you of the house?   110

BESS.

　　I am, sir.

CARROL.

　　In what place?

BESS.

　　I draw.

CARROL.

　　Beer, do you not? You are some tapstress.

SPENCER.

　　Sir, the worst character you can bestow   *better than that*   115
　　Upon the maid is to draw wine.

CARROL.

　　She would draw none to us.
　　Perhaps she keeps a rundlet for your taste,
　　Which none but you must pierce.

2 CAPTAIN.   I pray be civil.

SPENCER.

　　I know not, gentlemen, what your intents be,   120
　　Nor do I fear or care. This is my room;

---

112. *In . . . place?*] how are you occupied?
118. *rundlet*] cask of liquor (here with indecent double meaning).

－14－

And if you bear you, as you seem in show,
Like gentlemen, sit and be sociable.

CARROL.

We will.— [*To* Bess.] Minx, by your leave. Remove, I say.

SPENCER.

She shall not stir.

CARROL.   How, sir?

SPENCER.   No, sir. Could you   125
Outface the devil, we do not fear your roaring.

CARROL.

Though you may be companion with a drudge,
It is not fit she should have place by us.—
About your business, housewife.

SPENCER.   She is worthy
The place as the best here, and she shall keep't.   *org* 130

CARROL.

You lie.   *They bustle.* Carrol *slain.*

GOODLACK.

The gentleman's slain; away!

BESS.

Oh heaven, what have you done?

GOODLACK.

Undone thyself and me too. Come away.

                    [*Exeunt* Spencer *and* Goodlack.]

BESS.

Oh sad misfortune, I shall lose him ever.—   135
What, are you men or milksops? Stand you still
Senseless as stones, and see your friend in danger
To expire his last?

1 CAPTAIN.   Tush, all our help's in vain.

2 CAPTAIN.   *lo|*
This is the fruit of whores. This mischief came
Through thee.

BESS.   It grew first from your incivility.   140

---

126. *roaring*] blustering, the allusion being to the traditional depiction of devils in miracle plays as well as to the characteristics of the "roaring boy," the Elizabethan swaggerer or bully (cf. II.i.78).

127. *companion*] used slightingly, like "fellow, boy."

129. *housewife*] i.e., hussy.

1 CAPTAIN.

    Lend me a hand to lift his body hence.

    It was a fatal business.   *Exeunt* Captains [*with body*].

Enter the two Drawers.

1 DRAWER.

    One call my master; another fetch the constable. Here's a

    man kill'd in the room.

2 DRAWER.

    How, a man kill'd, say'st thou? Is all paid?   145

1 DRAWER.

    How fell they out, canst thou tell?

2 DRAWER.

    Sure, about this bold Bettrice. 'Tis not so much for the death

    of the man, but how shall we come by our reckoning?

                                     Exeunt Drawers.

BESS.

    What shall become of me, of all lost creatures

    The most infortunate? My innocence   150

    Hath been the cause of blood, and I am now

    Purpled with murder, though not within compass

    Of the law's severe censure; but, which most

    Adds unto my affliction, I by this

    Have lost so worthy and approv'd a friend,   155

    Whom to redeem from exile I would give

    All that's without and in me.

Enter Forset.

FORSET.

    Your name's Bess Bridges?

BESS.   An unfortunate maid,

    Known by that name too well in Plymouth here.

    Your business, sir, with me?   160

FORSET.

    Know you this ring?

BESS.   I do; it is my Spencer's.

    I know withal you are his trusty friend,

---

147. *bold Bettrice*] a forward woman. Cf. *The Batchelars Banquet*, 1603, ed.
F. P. Wilson (1929), pp. 22–23.

    To whom he would commit it. Speak; how fares he?
    Is he in freedom, know ye?

FORSET.   He's in health
    Of body, though in mind somewhat perplex'd   165
    For this late mischief happened.

BESS.   Is he fled
    And freed from danger?

FORSET.   Neither. By this token
    He lovingly commends him to you, Bess,
    And prays you when 'tis dark meet him o'th' Hoe
    Near to the new-made fort, where he'll attend you,   170
    Before he flies to take a kind farewell.
    There's only Goodlack in his company;
    He entreats you not to fail him.

BESS.

    Tell him from me, I'll come, I'll run, I'll fly,
    Stand death before me, were I sure to die.   175

                        Exit [*with* Forset].

[I.iii]   *Enter* Spencer *and* Goodlack.

GOODLACK.

    You are too full of passion.

SPENCER.   Canst thou blame me,
    To have the guilt of murder burden me;
    And next, my life in hazard to a death
    So ignominious; last, to lose a love
    So sweet, so fair, so am'rous, and so chaste;   5
    And all these at an instant? Art thou sure
    Carrol is dead?

GOODLACK.   I can believe no less.
    You hit him in the very speeding place.

SPENCER.

    Oh, but the last of these sits near'st my heart.

GOODLACK.

    Sir, be advis'd by me.   10
    Try her before you trust her. She perchance

---

169. *Hoe*] a bluff overlooking the sea, in Plymouth.
[I.iii]
  8. *speeding*] deadly.

-17-

May take th'advantage of your hopeful fortunes,
But when she finds you subject to distress
And casualty, her flattering love may die
With your deceased hopes.

SPENCER.   Thou counsel'st well.   15
I'll put her to the test and utmost trial
Before I trust her further. Here she comes.

Enter Forset, *and* Bess *with a bag.*

FORSET.
I have done my message, sir.

BESS.
Fear not, sweet Spencer; we are now alone,
And thou art sanctuar'd in these mine arms.   20

GOODLACK.
While these confer we'll sentinel their safety.
This place I'll guard.

FORSET.   I this.

BESS.   Are you not hurt?
Or your skin ras'd with his offensive steel?
How is it with you?

SPENCER.   Bess, all my afflictions
Are that I must leave thee. Thou know'st withal   25
My extreme necessity and that the fear
Of a most scandalous death doth force me hence.
I am not near my country, and to stay
For new supply from thence might deeply engage me
To desperate hazard.

BESS.   Is it coin you want?   30
Here is the hundred pound you gave me late.
Use that, beside what I have stor'd and sav'd,
Which makes it fifty more. Were it ten thousand,
Nay, a whole million, Spencer, all were thine.

SPENCER.
No, what thou hast, keep still; 'tis all thine own.   35
Here be my keys; my trunks take to thy charge.
Such gold fit for transportage as I have,

15. With] *Shepherd; not in Q.*   29. For] *Collier; From Q.*

23. *ras'd*] slashed.

I'll bear along; the rest are freely thine.
Money, apparel, and what else thou find'st
Perhaps worth my bequest and thy receiving,   40
I make thee mistress of.

BESS.   Before I doted,
But now you strive to have me ecstasied.
What would you have me do in which t'express
My zeal to you?

SPENCER.   My picture I enjoin
Thee to keep ever, which in my chamber hangs,   45
For when thou part'st with that, thou losest me.

BESS.
My soul may from my body be divorc'd,
But never that from me.

SPENCER.
I have a house in Foy, a tavern call'd
The Windmill, that I freely give thee too,   50
And thither if I live I'll send to thee.

BESS.
So soon as I have cast my reckonings up
And made even with my master, I'll not fail
To visit Foy in Cornwall. Is there else
Aught that you will enjoin me?

SPENCER.   Thou art fair;   55
Join to thy beauty virtue. Many suitors
I know will tempt thee; beauty's a shrewd bait,
But unto that if thou add'st chastity,
Thou shalt o'ercome all scandal. Time calls hence;
We now must part.   60

BESS.
Oh that I had the power to make time lame,
To stay the stars or make the moon stand still
That future day might never haste thy flight.
I could dwell here forever in thine arms

44–45. My . . . hangs,] *this edn.*;
Which in my chamber hangs,/ My
picture, I injoyne thee to keepe ever,
Q and modern edns., except I enjoin
thee to keep/ Ever my picture,
which in my chamber hangs;
Verity.

49. *Foy*] Fowey, a small Cornish port.

And wish it always night.   65

SPENCER.

We trifle hours. Farewell.

BESS.   First take this ring.
'Twas the first token of my constant love
That pass'd betwixt us. When I see this next
And not my Spencer, I shall think thee dead;
For till death part thy body from thy soul,   70
I know thou wilt not part with it.

SPENCER.

Swear for me, Bess, for thou may'st safely do't.
Once more farewell; at Foy thou shalt hear from me.

BESS.

There's not a word that hath a parting sound
Which through mine ears shrills not immediate death.   75
I shall not live to lose thee.

FORSET.

Best be gone; for hark, I hear some tread.

SPENCER.

A thousand farewells are in one contracted.
Captain, away!   *Exeunt* Spencer *and* Goodlack.

BESS.

Oh, I shall die.   80

FORSET.

What mean you, Bess? Will you betray your friend,
Or call my name in question? Sweet, look up.

BESS.

Hah, is my Spencer gone?

FORSET.   With speed towards Foy,
There to take ship for Fayal.

BESS.

Let me recollect myself   85
And what he left in charge, virtue and chastity;
Next, with all sudden expedition
Prepare for Foy. All these will I conserve

79. S.D. *Exeunt*] *Collier; Exit Q*.

---

72. *Swear . . . me*] answer for me (i.e., you may take your oath that I will
not part with the ring).
84. *Fayal*] an island in the Azores.

And keep them strictly as I would my life.
Plymouth, farewell; in Cornwall I will prove   90
A second fortune and forever mourn
Until I see my Spencer's safe return.   [*Exeunt.*]

[I.iv] *Hautboys. A dumb show. Enter General, Captains, the Mayor* [*of Plymouth*]. *Petitioners the other way with papers, amongst these the* Drawers. *The General gives them bags of money. All go off saving the two* Drawers.

1 DRAWER.

'Tis well yet we have gotten all the money due to my master.
It is the commonest thing that can be for these captains to
score and to score, but when the scores are to be paid, *non est
inventus.*

2 DRAWER.

'Tis ordinary amongst gallants nowadays, who had rather   5
swear forty oaths than only this one oath: "God let me never
be trusted."

1 DRAWER.

But if the captains would follow the noble mind of the
general, before night there would not be one score owing in
Plymouth.   10

2 DRAWER.

Little knows Bess that my master hath got in these desperate
debts. But she hath cast up her accounts and is gone.

1 DRAWER.

Whither, canst thou tell?

2 DRAWER.

They say to keep a tavern in Foy and that Mr. Spencer hath
given her a stock to set up for herself. Well, howsoever, I am   15
glad though he kill'd the man, we have got our money. [*Exeunt.*]

Explicit Actus primus.

[II.i]   *Enter* Forset *and* Roughman.

FORSET.

In your time have you seen a sweeter creature?

12. accounts] *possibly* account *in* Q.

2–3. *to score and to score*] to run up bill after bill.
3–4. *non est inventus*] he is not to be found (inscribed on warrants, etc.,
when the person on whom they were to be served could not be located).

ROUGHMAN.

Some week or thereabouts.

FORSET.

And in that small time she hath almost undone all the other
taverns. The gallants make no rendezvous now but at the
Windmill.   5

ROUGHMAN.

Spite of them, I'll have her. It shall cost me the setting on,
but I'll have her.

FORSET.

Why, do you think she is so easily won?

ROUGHMAN.

Easily or not, I'll bid as fair and far as any man within
twenty miles of my head, but I will put her to the squeak.   10

FORSET.

They say there are knights' sons already come as suitors to
her.

ROUGHMAN.

'Tis like enough some younger brothers, and so I intend to
make them.

FORSET.

If these doings hold, she will grow rich in short time.   15

ROUGHMAN.

There shall be doings that shall make this Windmill my
grand seat, my mansion, my palace, and my Constantinople.

Enter Bess Bridges *like a mistress, and* Clem.

FORSET.

Here she comes. Observe how modestly she bears herself.

ROUGHMAN.

I must know of what burden this vessel is. I shall not bear

---

6. *cost . . . on*] cost me dear (*OED*, with query).

10. *put . . . squeak*] cause her to squeak (i.e., press her hard).

13. *'Tis . . . enough*] no doubt.

13–14. *younger . . . them*] Because estates ordinarily passed from father to
eldest son, younger brothers had to make their own fortunes. Roughman
means that the knights' sons who are courting Bess are after her money and
that he intends further to disinherit them by marrying her himself.

19–21. *I must . . . carriage*] Forset (l. 18) has said, "See how modestly
she behaves herself." Roughman extends *bear* to *burden*, meaning "I must

with her till she bear with me, and till then I cannot report   20
her for a woman of good carriage.

BESS.

Your old master that dwelt here before my coming hath
turn'd over your years to me.

CLEM.

Right, forsooth. Before he was a vintner, he was a shoemaker
and left two or three turnovers more besides myself.   25

BESS.

How long hast thou to serve?

CLEM.

But eleven years next grass, and then I am in hope of my
freedom. For by that time I shall be at full age.

BESS.

How old art thou now?

CLEM.

Forsooth, newly come into my teens. I have scrap'd tren-   30
chers this two years, and the next vintage I hope to be bar
boy.

BESS.

What's thy name?

CLEM.

My name is Clem. My father was a baker and, by the report
of his neighbors, as honest a man as ever lived by bread.   35

BESS.

And where dwelt he?

---

know how rich she is" (a vessel's *burden* is her cargo), and continues with a
series of conventional puns: *I shall . . . me* = I shall not favor her (a ship
bears with the port toward which she sails) until she (1) favors me, (2) supports me financially, (3) supports me physically, goes to bed with me.
Carriage means (1) general deportment, (2) manner of acting in a specific
instance, here with sexual allusion, and (3) ability to carry cargo or wealth.

23. *your years*] the term of your apprenticeship.

25. *turnovers*] (1) apprentices "whose indentures are transferred to another
master on the retirement or failure of his original one" (*OED*); (2) welts of
cork shoes.

27. *eleven years*] The Statute of Artificers of 1563 prescribed a term of
apprenticeship of at least seven years to end, in corporate towns, when the
apprentice was twenty-four years old. If Clem is now thirteen (*newly come
into [his] teens*, l. 30), he will be twenty-four in eleven years, at which time he
will gain his freedom (be granted the right to practice his trade at hire).

CLEM.

>Below here in the next crooked street, at the sign of the Leg.
>He was nothing so tall as I, but a little wee man and
>somewhat huck'd-back'd.

BESS.

>He was once constable?   40

CLEM.

>He was indeed, and in that one year of his reign, I have
>heard them say, he bolted and sifted out more business than
>others in that office in many years before him.

BESS.

>How long is't since he died?

CLEM.

>Marry, the last dear year. For when corn grew to be at an   45
>high rate, my father never dowed after.

BESS.

>I think I have heard of him.

CLEM.

>Then I am sure you have heard he was an honest neighbor
>and one that never lov'd to be meal-mouth'd.

BESS.

>Well, sirrah, prove an honest servant, and you shall find me   50
>your good mistress. What company is in the Mermaid?

CLEM.

>There be four sea captains. I believe they be little better than
>spirats, they are so flush of their ruddocks.

---

37. *sign . . . Leg*] The joke turns on several allusions: the Leg would be an
appropriate sign for a bootmaker, not a baker (cf. *2 Henry IV*, II.iv.251);
knock-knees were known as baker-legs; and there may have been a tavern
at the sign of the Leg as there was some fifty years later (see Henry C.
Shelley, *Inns and Taverns of Old London* [1923], p. 141).

39. *huck'd-back'd*] hump-backed.

42. *bolted . . . out*] Clem plays on terms appropriate to both the baker's
and the constable's offices. The baker *bolts* (sieves) and *sifts out* his materials;
the constable *bolts* (locks up) felons and *sifts out* (investigates) crimes.

45. *dear year*] a year in which the price of grain was high.

46. *dowed*] (1) prospered; (2) worked in dough.

53. *spirats*] Clem's word for "pirates."

53. *ruddocks*] gold coins, money (perhaps with allusion also to the captains'
ruddy complexions).

BESS.

No matter; we will take no note of them. Here they vent
many brave commodities by which some gain accrues.   55
Th'are my good customers, and still return me profit.

CLEM.

Wot you what, mistress, how the two sailors would have
served me that call'd for the pound and half of cheese?

BESS.

How was it, Clem?

CLEM.

When I brought them a reckoning, they would have had me   60
to have scor'd it up. They took me for a simple gull indeed,
that would have had me to have taken chalk for cheese.

BESS.

Well, go wait upon the captains; see them want no wine.

CLEM.

Nor reckoning neither; take my word, mistress.

ROUGHMAN.

She's now at leisure; I'll to her.—   65
Lady, what gentlemen are those above?

BESS.

Sir, they are such as please to be my guests,
And they are kindly welcome.

ROUGHMAN.   Give me their names.

BESS.

You may go search the church book where they were
    christen'd;
There you perhaps may learn them.

ROUGHMAN.   Minion, how?   [Seizes her.]   70

FORSET.

Fie, fie, you are too rude with this fair creature
That no way seeks t'offend you.

BESS.   Pray, hands off.

---

54. *vent*] vend, sell.   55. *brave*] valuable.
55. *accrues*] advantages, profits.   57. *Wot*] know.
61. *scor'd it up*] put it on account (patrons' accounts were kept by chalk
marks on a slate or door; hence, the proverbial *chalk for cheese*, l. 62).
61. *gull*] (1) dupe; (2) the marine bird, who would be stupider than usual
if he mistook chalk for cheese.
70. *Minion*] hussy.

ROUGHMAN.

I tell thee, maid, wife, or whate'er thou beest,
No man shall enter here but by my leave.
Come, let's be more familiar.

BESS.   'Las, goodman.   75

ROUGHMAN.

Why, know'st thou whom thou slight'st? I am Roughman,
The only approved gallant of these parts,
A man of whom the roarers stand in awe,
And must not be put off.

BESS.

I never yet heard man so praise himself,   80
But prov'd in th'end a coward.

ROUGHMAN.   Coward, Bess?

You will offend me, raise in me that fury
Your beauty cannot calm. Go to, no more;
Your language is too harsh and peremptory.
Pray let me hear no more on't. I tell thee   85
That quiet day scarce pass'd me these seven years
I have not crack'd a weapon in some fray,
And will you move my spleen?

FORSET.   What, threat a woman?

BESS.

Sir, if you thus persist to wrong my house,
Disturb my guests, and nightly domineer,   90
To put my friends from patience, I'll complain
And right myself before the magistrate.
Can we not live in compass of the law,
But must be swagger'd out on't?

ROUGHMAN.   Go to, wench.

I wish thee well, think on't; there's good for thee   95
Stor'd in my breast, and when I come in place
I must have no man to offend mine eye.
My love can brook no rivals. For this time
I am content your captains shall have peace,

---

75. *goodman*] title for one beneath the rank of gentleman (used contemptuously here to imply want of manners).

77. *approved*] proved, tested, esteemed.

83. *Go to*] i.e., "come, come," a mild remonstrance.

96. *come in place*] appear (as your suitor).

But must not be us'd to't.

BESS.   Sir, if you come   100
Like other free and civil gentlemen,
Y'are welcome; otherwise my doors are barr'd you.

ROUGHMAN.
That's my good girl.
I have fortunes laid up for thee; what I have
Command it as thine own. Go to; be wise.   105

BESS.
Well, I shall study for't.

ROUGHMAN.
Consider on't. Farewell.   *Exit* [*with* Forset].

BESS.
My mind suggests me that this prating fellow
Is some notorious coward. If he persist,
I have a trick to try what mettle's in him.   110

Enter Clem.

What news with you?

CLEM.
I am now going to carry the captains a reck'ning.

BESS.
And what's the sum?

CLEM.
Let me see—eight shillings and sixpence.

BESS.
How can you make that good? Write them a bill.   115

CLEM.
I'll watch them for that; 'tis no time of night to use our bills.
The gentlemen are no dwarfs, and with one word of my
mouth I can tell them what is to *be-tall*.

BESS.
How comes it to so much?

CLEM.
Imprimis, six quarts of wine at seven pence the quart—seven 120
sixpences.

---

101. *free*] generous in manner, liberal.
116. *bills*] Clem shifts the meaning of *bill* (l. 115) to "halberd," a weapon
with which the *watch* (l. 116) was armed.
118. *be-tall*] from Dutch *betalen*, to pay, with obvious pun.

BESS.

Why dost thou reckon it so?

CLEM.

Because as they came in by hab nab, so I will bring them in
a reck'ning at six and at sevens.

BESS.

Well, wine—three shillings and sixpence.　　　　　125

CLEM.

And what wants that of ten groats?

BESS.

'Tis two pence over.

CLEM.

Then put six pence more to it and make it four shillings wine,
though you bate it them in their meat.

BESS.

Why so, I prithee?　　　　　130

CLEM.

Because of the old proverb *What they want in meat, let them
take out in drink.* Then for twelve pennyworth of anchovies—
eighteen pence.

BESS.

How can that be?

CLEM.

Marry, very well, mistress: twelve pence anchovies and 135
sixpence oil and vinegar. Nay, they shall have a saucy
reckoning.

BESS.

And what for the other half-crown?

CLEM.

Bread, beer, salt, napkins, trenchers, one thing with
another; so the *summa totalis* is—eight shillings and sixpence. 140

BESS.

Well, take the reckoning from the bar.

CLEM.

What needs that forsooth? The gentlemen seem to be high-

125. three . . . sixpence] *Verity*; 3s, 　140. eight . . . sixpence] *Collier*; 8s,
6d *Q*. 　　　　　　　　　　　　　　　6d *Q*.

123. *by hab nab*] confusedly, at random.
126. *groats*] coins worth four pence.
129. *bate*] reduce.　　　142–143. *high-flown*] intoxicated.

flown already. Send them in but another pottle of sack, and
they will cast up the reckoning of themselves. Yes, I'll about
it.   [*Exit.*] 145

BESS.

Were I not with so many suitors pester'd
And might I enjoy my Spencer, what a sweet,
Contented life were this? For money flows
And my gain's great. But to my Roughman next.
I have a trick to try what spirit's in him;   150
It shall be my next business. In this passion
For my dear Spencer, I propose me this:
'Mongst many sorrows some mirth's not amiss.   *Exit.*

[II.ii]   *Enter* Spencer *and* Goodlack.

GOODLACK.

What were you thinking, sir?

SPENCER.

Troth, of the world: what any man should see in't to be in
love with it.

GOODLACK.

The reason of your meditation?

SPENCER.

To imagine that in the same instant that one forfeits all his   5
estate, another enters upon a rich possession. As one goes to
the church to be married, another is hurried to the gallows
to be hang'd, the last having no feeling of the first man's joy
nor the first of the last man's misery. At the same time that
one lies tortured upon the rack, another lies tumbling with   10
his mistress over head and ears in down and feathers. This
when I truly consider, I cannot but wonder why any fortune
should make a man ecstasied.

GOODLACK.

You give yourself too much to melancholy.

146. many] *Shepherd* (*Dyce's notes*);
my Q.

---

144. *cast up*] (1) add up; (2) vomit.
[II.ii]
10. *rack*] an instrument of torture that stretched the joints of the one
strapped to it.

SPENCER.

These are my maxims, and were they as faithfully practiced   15
by others as truly apprehended by me, we should have less
oppression and more charity.

Enter the two Captains *that were before.*

1 CAPTAIN.
Make good thy words.

2 CAPTAIN   I say thou hast injur'd me.

1 CAPTAIN.
Tell me wherein.

2 CAPTAIN.   When we assaulted Fayal,
And I had by the general's command   20
The onset, and with danger of my person
Enforc'd the Spaniard to a swift retreat
And beat them from their fort, thou when thou saw'st
All fear and danger past, mad'st up with me
To share that honor which was sole mine own   25
And never ventur'd shot for't or e'er came
Where bullet graz'd.

SPENCER.   See, Captain, a fray towards.
Let's, if we can, atone this difference.

GOODLACK.
Content.

1 CAPTAIN.
I'll prove it with my sword   30
That though thou had'st the foremost place in field
And I the second, yet my company
Was equal in the entry of the fort.
My sword was that day drawn as soon as thine,
And that poor honor which I won that day   35
Was but my merit.

2 CAPTAIN.   Wrong me palpably
And justify the same?

SPENCER.   You shall not fight.

1 CAPTAIN.
Why, sir, who made you first a justicer

---

24. *mad'st up*] caught up.
27. *towards*] impending.   38. *justicer*] magistrate.

And taught you that word "shall"? You are no general
Or, if you be, pray show us your commission.   40

SPENCER.

Sir, you have no commission but my counsel,
And that I'll show you freely.

2 CAPTAIN.   'Tis some chaplain.

1 CAPTAIN.

I do not like his text.

GOODLACK.

Let's beat their weapons down.

1 CAPTAIN.

I'll aim at him that offers to divide us!   [*They fight.*]   45

2 CAPTAIN.

Pox of these part-frays! See, I am wounded
By beating down my weapon.

GOODLACK.

How fares my friend?

SPENCER.

You sought for blood, and, gentlemen, you have it.
Let mine appease you; I am hurt to death.   50

1 CAPTAIN.

My rage converts to pity that this gentleman
Shall suffer for his goodness.

GOODLACK.   Noble friend,
I will revenge thy death.

SPENCER.   He is no friend
That murmurs such a thought. —Oh, gentlemen,
I kill'd a man in Plymouth and by you   55
Am slain in Fayal. Carrol fell by me,
And I fall by a Spencer. Heav'n is just
And will not suffer murder unreveng'd.
Heaven pardon me, as I forgive you both.
Shift for yourselves. Away!

2 CAPTAIN.   We saw him die,   60
But grieve you should so perish.

SPENCER.   Note heaven's justice,
And henceforth make that use on't. I shall faint.

---

41. *you*] Collier first suggested emending to *I*, but "you have" means
"with respect to you" or "there is for you."

1 CAPTAIN.

    Short farewells now must serve. If thou surviv'st,
    Live to thine honor, but if thou expir'st,
    Heaven take thy soul to mercy.   *Exeunt* [Captains].

SPENCER.   I bleed much;   65

    I must go seek a surgeon.

GOODLACK.   Sir, how cheer you?

SPENCER.

    Like one that's bound upon a new adventure
    To th'other world. Yet thus much, worthy friend,
    Let me entreat you, since I understand
    The fleet is bound for England: take your occasion   70
    To ship yourself, and when you come to Foy,
    Kindly commend me to my dearest Bess.
    Thou shalt receive a will, in which I have
    Possess'd her of five hundred pounds a year.

GOODLACK.

    A noble legacy.   75

SPENCER.

    The rest I have bestow'd amongst my friends,
    Only reserving a bare hundred pounds
    To see me honestly and well interr'd.

GOODLACK.

    I shall perform your trust as carefully
    As to my father, breath'd he.

SPENCER.   Mark me, Captain.   80

    Her legacy I give with this proviso:
    If at thy arrival where my Bess remains,
    Thou find'st her well reported, free from scandal,
    My will stands firm; but if thou hear'st her branded
    For loose behavior or immodest life,   85
    What she should have I here bestow on thee,
    It is thine own. But as thou lov'st thy soul
    Deal faithfully betwixt my Bess and me.

GOODLACK.

    Else let me die a prodigy.

---

    89. *prodigy*] monster (in general, anything amazing, marvellous, very extraordinary).

SPENCER.

This ring was hers. That, be she loose or chaste,   90
Being her own, restore her; she will know it,
And doubtless she deserves it. Oh, my memory!
What, had I quite forgot? She hath my picture.

GOODLACK.

And what of that?

SPENCER.

If she be rank'd amongst the loose and lewd,   95
Take it away (I hold it much undecent
A whore should ha't in keeping), but if constant,
Let her enjoy it. This my will perform
As thou art just and honest.

GOODLACK.   Sense else forsake me.

SPENCER.

Now lead me to my chamber. All's made even: 100
My peace with earth and my atone with heaven.   [*Exeunt.*]

[II.iii]   *Enter* Bess Bridges *like a page with a sword, and* Clem.

BESS.

But that I know my mother to be chaste,
I'd swear some soldier got me.

CLEM.

It may be many a soldier's buff jerkin came out of your
father's tan-fat.

BESS.

Methinks I have a manly spirit in me   5
In this man's habit.

CLEM.

Now am not I of many men's minds, for if you should do me
wrong, I should not kill you, though I took you pissing against
a wall.

BESS.

Methinks I could be valiant on the sudden   10

100. made] *Collier*; mads *Q*.

2. *got*] begot.
4. *fat*] vat. The substitution of "f" for "v", a feature of Southern dialect,
was conventional in the speech of stage yokels.

-33-

And meet a man i'th' field.
I could do all that I have heard discours'd
Of Mary Ambree or Westminster's Long Meg.

CLEM.

What Mary Ambree was I cannot tell, but unless you were
taller you will come short of Long Meg.   15

BESS.

Of all thy fellows thee I only trust
And charge thee to be secret.

CLEM.

I am bound in my indentures to keep my master's secrets,
and should I find a man in bed with you, I would not tell.

BESS.

Begone, sir, but no words, as you esteem my favor.   20

CLEM.

But, mistress, I could wish you to look to your long seams;
fights are dangerous. But am not I in a sweet taking, think
you?

BESS.

I prithee why?

CLEM.

Why, if you should swagger and kill anybody, I, being a   25
vintner, should be call'd to the bar.   [*Exit.*]

BESS.

Let none condemn me of immodesty
Because I try the courage of a man
Who on my soul's a coward; beats my servants,

---

13. *Mary Ambree . . . Long Meg*] popular heroines of chapbook and ballad,
who, like Bess, donned male attire and engaged in high adventure. Mary
Ambree, according to a ballad in Percy's *Reliques*, fought against the
Spanish at the siege of Ghent, 1584, to revenge the death of her English
lover. She was often alluded to: by Jonson (*Epicoene*, IV.ii), Marston
(*Antonio and Mellida*, I.i), Fletcher (*Scornful Lady*, V.iv). Long Meg was
known for physical strength and fighting spirit; she was at one point a
servant in and later mistress of a tavern, and among other exploits decapi-
tated a French champion before the walls of Boulogne. Her story was told in
a chapbook of 1582.
15. *taller*] bolder, with obvious pun.
21. *long seams*] the seams of her hose.
22. *sweet taking*] good situation.
26. *call'd . . . bar*] (1) as a bartender; (2) as a lawyer.

Cuffs them, and, as they pass by him, kicks my maids;   30
Nay, domineers over me, making himself
Lord o'er my house and household. Yesternight
I heard him make appointment on some business
To pass alone this way. I'll venture fair
But I will try what's in him.   [*Withdraws.*]   35

Enter Roughman *and* Forset.

FORSET.

Sir, I can now no further; weighty business
Calls me away.

ROUGHMAN.   Why, at your pleasure then,
Yet I could wish that ere I pass'd this field
That I could meet some Hector, so your eyes
Might witness what myself have oft repeated,   40
Namely, that I am valiant.

FORSET.

Sir, no doubt; but now I am in haste. Farewell.   [*Exit.*]

ROUGHMAN.

How many times brave words bear out a man!
For if he can but make a noise, he's fear'd.
To talk of frays, although he ne'er had heart   45
To face a man in field, that's a brave fellow.
I have been valiant, I must needs confess,
In street and tavern, where there have been men
Ready to part the fray; but for the fields,
They are too cold to fight in.   50

BESS.

You are a villain, a coward; and you lie.   [*Strikes him.*]

ROUGHMAN.

You wrong me, I protest. Sweet courteous gentleman,

---

34. *venture fair*] risk all.
39. *Hector*] fighter, bully; cf. *Trojan* (III.i.5).
51. *You . . . lie*] Bess is huddling together several features of the formal
code of honor supposed to be observed by gentlemen. By calling Roughman
a villain and a coward, she has given him an injury in word; to this he
should reply, "You lie," whereupon she should challenge him. By striking
him she has given him an injury in deed; he should say, "You have abused
me," to which she should answer, "You lie," whereupon he should challenge
her. (See *Vincentio Saviolo his Practice* [1595], R3ᵛ–4.) Carrol gives Spencer the
lie at I.ii.131.

I never did you wrong.

BESS.   Wilt tell me that?

Draw forth thy coward sword, and suddenly,

Or as I am a man I'll run thee through   55

And leave thee dead i'th' field.

ROUGHMAN.

Hold, as you are a gentleman. I have ta'en an oath

I will not fight today.

BESS.

Th'ast took a blow already and the lie;

Will not both these enrage thee?   60

ROUGHMAN.

No, would you give the bastinado too,

I will not break mine oath.

BESS.   Oh, your name's Roughman.

No day doth pass you but you hurt or kill.

Is this out of your calendar?

ROUGHMAN.   I? You are deceiv'd.

I ne'er drew sword in anger, I protest,   65

Unless it were upon some poor, weak fellow

That ne'er wore steel about him.

BESS.   Throw your sword.

ROUGHMAN.

Here, sweet young sir; but as you are a gentleman,

Do not impair mine honor.

BESS.   Tie that shoe.

ROUGHMAN.

I shall, sir.

BESS.   Untruss that point.   70

ROUGHMAN.

Anything this day to save mine oath.

BESS.

Enough. Yet not enough. Lie down,

Till I stride o'er thee.

ROUGHMAN.   Sweet sir, anything.

---

61. *the bastinado*] a beating, or, more specifically, whipping the soles of the feet as a torture.

64. *this out*] i.e., this day left out.

70. *point*] lace attaching doublet to hose.

BESS.

    Rise; thou hast leave. Now, Roughman, thou art blest.
    This day thy life is sav'd; look to the rest.   75
    Take back thy sword.

ROUGHMAN.

    Oh, you are generous; honor me so much
    As let me know to whom I owe my life.

BESS.

    I am Bess Bridges' brother.

ROUGHMAN.   Still methought
    That you were something-like her.

BESS.   And I have heard   80
    You domineer and revel in her house,
    Control her servants, and abuse her guests,
    Which if I ever shall hereafter hear,
    Thou art but a dead man.

ROUGHMAN.

    She never told me of a brother living,   85
    But you have power to sway me.

BESS.

    But for I see you are a gentleman,
    I am content this once to let you pass;
    But if I find you fall into relapse,
    The second's far more dangerous.

ROUGHMAN.   I shall fear it.   90
    Sir, will you take the wine?

BESS.   I am for London,
    And for these two terms cannot make return;
    But if you see my sister, you may say
    I was in health.

ROUGHMAN [*aside*].   Too well, the devil take you!

BESS.

    Pray use her well, and at my coming back   95
    I'll ask for your acquaintance. Now, farewell.   [*Exit.*]

---

  82. *Control*] reprove.
  92. *terms*] periods "appointed for the sitting of certain courts of law, or
for the instruction or study in a university or school" (*OED*); there were
four: Hilary, Easter, Trinity, and Michaelmas.

ROUGHMAN.

>None saw't. He's gone for London; I am unhurt.
>Then who shall publish this disgrace abroad?
>One man's no slander, should he speak his worst.
>My tongue's as loud as his, but in this country   100
>Both of more fame and credit. Should we contest,
>I can outface the proudest. This is then
>My comfort: Roughman, thou art still the same,
>For a disgrace not seen is held no shame.   [*Exit.*]

[II.iv]   *Enter two* Sailors.

1 SAILOR.

>Aboard, aboard! The wind stands fair for England;
>The ships have all weigh'd anchor.

2 SAILOR.

>A stiff gale blows from the shore.

                    Enter Captain Goodlack.

GOODLACK.

>The sailors call aboard, and I am forc'd
>To leave my friend now at the point of death,   5
>And cannot close his eyes. Here is the will.
>Now may I find yon tanner's daughter turn'd
>Unchaste or wanton, I shall gain by it
>Five hundred pounds a year. Here is good evidence.

1 SAILOR.

>Sir, will you take the long boat and aboard?   10

                    Enter a third Sailor.

GOODLACK.

>With all my heart.

3 SAILOR.   What, are you ready, mates?

1 SAILOR.

>We stay'd for you. Thou canst not tell who's dead?
>The great bell rung out now.

3 SAILOR.

>They say 'twas for one Spencer, who this night
>Died of a mortal wound.

---

6. *close his eyes*] i.e., be present at his death. (To close the eyes of the corpse
is a gesture of affectionate regard.)

GOODLACK.   My worthy friend.   15

    Unhappy man that cannot stay behind

    To do him his last rites. —Was his name Spencer?

3 SAILOR.

    Yes, sir; a gentleman of good account,

    And well known in the navy.

GOODLACK.

    This is the end of all mortality.   20

    It will be news unpleasing to his Bess.

    I cannot fare amiss, but long to see

    Whether these lands belong to her or me.   [*Exeunt.*]

[II.v]   *Enter* Spencer *and his* Surgeon.

SURGEON.

    Nay, fear not, sir; now you have scap'd this dressing,

    My life for yours.

SPENCER.   I thank thee, honest friend.

SURGEON.

    Sir, I can tell you news.

SPENCER.   What is't, I prithee?

SURGEON.

    There is a gentleman, one of your name,

    That died within this hour.   5

SPENCER.

    My name? What was he? Of what sickness died he?

SURGEON.

    No sickness, but a slight hurt in the body,

    Which showed at first no danger, but being search'd,

    He died at the third dressing.

SPENCER.

    At my third search I am in hope of life.   10

    The heavens are merciful.

SURGEON.   Sir, doubt not your recovery.

SPENCER.

    That hundred pound I had prepar'd t'expend

---

    2. *My . . . yours*] i.e., you are in no more danger than I am *or* I will stake my life on your survival.

    6. *What was he*] Who was he? What was his position or rank?

    8. *search'd*] probed.

          Upon mine own expected funeral,
          I for name sake will now bestow on his.
SURGEON.
          A noble resolution.   15
SPENCER.
          What ships are bound for England? I would gladly
          Venture to sea, though weak.
SURGEON.
          All bound that way are under sail already.
SPENCER.
          Here's no security,
          For when the beaten Spaniards shall return,   20
          They'll spoil whom they can find.
SURGEON.   We have a ship,
          Of which I am surgeon, that belongs unto
          A London merchant, now bound for Mamorah,
          A town in Barbary; please you to use that,
          You shall command free passage. Ten months hence   25
          We hope to visit England.
SPENCER.   Friend, I thank thee.
SURGEON.
          I'll bring you to the master, who I know
          Will entertain you gladly.
SPENCER.
          When I have seen the funeral rites perform'd
          To the dead body of my countryman   30
          And kinsman, I will take your courteous offer.
          England, no doubt, will hear news of my death.
          How Bess will take it is to me unknown.
          On her behavior I will build my fate,
          There raise my love or thence erect my hate. [*Exeunt.*] 35

                    Explicit Actus secundus.

[III.i]   *Enter* Roughman *and* Forset.

ROUGHMAN.
          Oh, y'are well met. Just as I prophesied,
          So it fell out.

1. S.P. ROUGHMAN] *Collier*; *Forset Q*.
_____

     21. *spoil*] despoil, pillage.

FORSET.

> As how, I pray?

ROUGHMAN.

> Had you but stay'd the crossing of one field,
> You had beheld a Hector, the boldest Trojan   5
> That ever Roughman met with.

FORSET.   Pray, what was he?

ROUGHMAN.

> You talk of Little Davy, Cutting Dick,
> And divers such; but tush, this hath no fellow.

FORSET.

> Of what stature and years was he?

ROUGHMAN.

> Indeed, I must confess he was no giant   10
> Nor above fifty; but he did bestir him,
> Was here and there and everywhere at once,
> That I was ne'er so put to't since the midwife
> First wrapp'd my head in linen. Let's to Bess.
> I'll tell her the whole project.   15

FORSET.

> Here's the house; we'll enter if you please.

ROUGHMAN.

> Where be these drawers—rascals, I should say—
> That will give no attendance?

Enter Clem.

CLEM.

> Anon, anon, sir; please you see a room. [*Aside.*]   What,
> you here again? Now we shall have such roaring.   20

ROUGHMAN.

> You, sirrah, call your mistress.

---

7. *Little Davy, Cutting Dick*] Apparently "contemporary bravos of note" (Verity), although specific information about them has disappeared. Dekker alludes to Little Davy in *News from Hell* and Jonson in *Bartholomew Fair* (Induction). "Cutter" was a cant word for "swaggerer," and Cutting Dick is several times referred to as though he were a well-known highwayman. In 1602 Henslowe recorded a payment to Heywood for additions to a play about him, and in *The Wise-Woman of Hogsden* (II.i) a character described as a "swaggering companion" is also referred to as "cutting Dick." Cf. V.ii.131, where this sense of *cutting* is punningly combined with the usual one.

CLEM.

    Yes, sir, I know it is my duty to call her mistress.

ROUGHMAN.

    See an the slave will stir!   [*Takes him by the ear.*]

CLEM.

    Yes, I do stir.

ROUGHMAN.

    Shall we have humors, sauce-box? You have ears; I'll teach   25
you prick-song.

CLEM.

    But you have now a wrong sow by the ear. I will call her.

ROUGHMAN.

    Do, sir; you had best.   [*Lets him go.*]

CLEM.

    If you were twenty Roughmans, if you lug me by the ears
again, I'll draw.   30

ROUGHMAN.

    Ha, what will you draw?

CLEM.

    The best wine in the house for your worship; and I would
call her, but I can assure you she is either not stirring or else
not in case.

ROUGHMAN.

    How not in case?   35

CLEM.

    I think she hath not her smock on, for I think I saw it lie at
her bed's head.

ROUGHMAN.

    What, drawers grow capricious?   [*Offers to strike him.*]

CLEM.

    Help, help!

---

    26. *prick-song*] literally, music sung from written notes, but here with a
quibble (*prick* = vex, torment).

    27. *wrong . . . ear*] "You take the wrong sow by the ear" (Tilley, S 685) =
you have made a silly mistake, undertaken business that will be hard to
manage.

    35. *in case*] (1) dressed; (2) in the event. Roughman understands the
second sense, which is unintelligible in this context, and so asks, "How not
in case?" whereupon Clem shifts to the first sense.

    38. *capricious*] witty.

Enter Bess Bridges.

BESS.

    What uproar's this? Shall we be never rid   40

    From these disturbances?

ROUGHMAN.   Why, how now, Bess?

    Is this your housewif'ry? When you are mine,

    I'll have you rise as early as the lark.

    Look to the bar yourself; these lazy rascals

    Will bring your state behindhand.

CLEM.   You lie, sir!   45

ROUGHMAN.

    How! Lie?

CLEM.

    Yes, sir, at the Raven in the High Street. I was at your

    lodging this morning for a pottle pot.

ROUGHMAN.

    You will about your business; must you here

    Stand gaping and idle?   [*Strikes him.*]

BESS.   You wrong me, sir,   50

    And tyrannize too much over my servants.

    I will have no man touch them but myself.

CLEM [*aside*].

    If I do not put ratsbane into his wine instead of sugar, say I

    am no true baker.   [*Exit.*]

ROUGHMAN.

    What, rise at noon?   55

    A man may fight a tall fray in a morning,

    And one of your best friends too be hack'd and mangled

    And almost cut to pieces, and you, fast

    Close in your bed, ne'er dream on't.

BESS.   Fought you this day?

ROUGHMAN.

    And ne'er was better put to't in my days.   60

---

    45. *bring . . . behindhand*] ruin you financially.

    54. *true baker*] Bakers were notorious for secretly substituting cheap or un-
savory materials in their products; hence, " 'Tis not the smallness of the
bread but the knavery of the baker" (Tilley, under Y 26) and " 'I will take
no leave of you,' quoth the baker to the pillory" (L 171).

    58–59. *fast/ Close*] fast asleep and secure.

BESS.

I pray, how was't?

ROUGHMAN.   Thus. As I pass'd yon fields—

Enter the Kitchenmaid.

MAID.

I pray, forsooth, what shall I reckon for the jowl of ling in the
Portcullis?

ROUGHMAN.

A pox upon your jowls, you kitchen stuff!
Go scour your skillets, pots, and dripping pans,   65
And interrupt not us.   [*Kicks at her.*]

MAID.

The devil take your ox-heels, you foul cod's-head! Must you
be kicking?

ROUGHMAN.

Minion, dare you scold?

MAID.

Yes, sir, and lay my ladle over your coxcomb.   [*Exit.*]   70

BESS.

I do not think that thou dar'st strike a man,
That swagger'st thus o'er women.

ROUGHMAN.   How now, Bess?

BESS.

Shall we be never quiet?

FORSET.   You are too rude.

ROUGHMAN.

Now I profess all patience.

BESS.   Then proceed.

ROUGHMAN.

Rising up early, minion, whilst you slept,   75
To cross yon field, I had but newly parted
With this my friend, but that I soon espied
A gallant fellow, and most strongly arm'd.
In the mid-field we met, and both being resolute,

---

62. *jowl of ling*] the head of a ling (a kind of fish).

67. *cod's-head*] blockhead.

70. *coxcomb*] stupid head (the coxcomb was the headdress of a professional
fool).

We justled for the wall.   80
BESS.
    Why, did there stand a wall in the mid-field?
ROUGHMAN.
    I meant strove for the way.
    Two such brave spirits meeting, straight both drew.

Enter Clem.

CLEM.
    The maid, forsooth, sent me to know whether you would
    have the shoulder of mutton roasted or sod.   85
ROUGHMAN.
    A mischief on your shoulders!   [*Strikes him.*]
CLEM.
    That's the way to make me never prove good porter.
BESS.
    You still heap wrongs on wrongs.
ROUGHMAN.   I was in fury
    To think upon the violence of that fight
    And could not stay my rage.
FORSET.   Once more proceed.   90
ROUGHMAN.
    Oh, had you seen two tilting meteors justle
    In the mid-region, with like fear and fury
    We two encounter'd. Not Briareus
    Could with his hundred hands have struck more thick.
    Blows came about my head; I took them still;   95
    Thrusts by my sides, 'twixt body and my arms;
    Yet still I put them by.
BESS [*aside*].
    When they were past, he put them by. —Go on.
    But in this fury what became of him?
ROUGHMAN.
    I think I paid him home; he's soundly maul'd.   100

---

    80. *justled . . . wall*] i.e., contended for the privilege of walking next to the
wall, the cleaner and safer path.
    85. *sod*] boiled.
    92. *mid-region*] the second of the three theoretical divisions of the atmos-
phere.
    93. *Briareus*] a sea-giant of Greek mythology who had a hundred arms.
    100. *paid him home*] gave him his deserts (*OED*).

I bosom'd him at every second thrust.

BESS.

Scap'd he with life?

ROUGHMAN.

Ay, that's my fear. If he recover this,
I'll never trust my sword more.

BESS.

Why fly you not if he be in such danger? 105

ROUGHMAN.

Because a witch once told me
I ne'er should die for murder.

BESS.   I believe thee.
But tell me, pray, was not this gallant fellow
A pretty, fair, young youth, about my years?

ROUGHMAN.

Even thereabout.

CLEM.   He was not fifty then. 110

BESS.

Much of my stature?

ROUGHMAN.   Much about your pitch.

CLEM.

He was no giant then.

BESS.

And wore a suit like this?

ROUGHMAN.   I half suspect.

BESS.

That gallant fellow,
So wounded and so mangled, was myself. 115
You base, white-liver'd slave! It was this shoe
That thou stoop'd to untie, untruss'd those points,
And like a beastly coward lay along
Till I strid over thee. Speak, was't not so?

ROUGHMAN.

It cannot be denied. 120

BESS.

Hare-hearted fellow, milksop, dost not blush?
Give me that rapier. I will make thee swear

---

103. *that's my fear*] i.e., I am afraid he did not.
111. *pitch*] height.

Thou shalt redeem this scorn thou hast incurr'd,
Or in this woman shape I'll cudgel thee
And beat thee through the streets.   125
As I am Bess, I'll do't.

ROUGHMAN.   Hold, hold! I swear—

BESS.

Dare not to enter at my door till then.

ROUGHMAN.

Shame confounds me quite.

BESS.

That shame redeem; perhaps we'll do thee grace.
I love the valiant, but despise the base.   *Exit.* 130

CLEM.

Will you be kick'd, sir?

ROUGHMAN.   She hath waken'd me
And kindled that dead fire of courage in me
Which all this while hath slept. To spare my flesh
And wound my fame, what is't? I will not rest
Till by some valiant deed I have made good   135
All my disgraces past. I'll cross the street
And strike the next brave fellow that I meet.

FORSET.

I am bound to see the end on't.

ROUGHMAN.   Are you, sir?

Beats off Forset.

[III.ii]   *Enter* Mayor of Foy, *an* Alderman, *and* Servant.

MAYOR.

Believe me, sir, she bears herself so well
No man can justly blame her; and I wonder,
Being a single woman as she is
And living in an house of such resort,
She is no more distasted.

ALDERMAN.   The best gentlemen   5
The country yields become her daily guests.
Sure, sir, I think she's rich.

---

5. *distasted*] disliked, held to be offensive.

MAYOR.

    Thus much I know: would I could buy her state
    Were't for a brace of thousands.   *A shot.*

ALDERMAN.

    'Twas said a ship is now put into harbor.   10
    Know whence she is.

SERVANT.   I'll bring news from the quay.   [*Exit.*]

MAYOR.

    To tell you true, sir, I could wish a match
    Betwixt her and mine own and only son,
    And stretch my purse too upon that condition.

ALDERMAN.

    Please you, I'll motion it.   15

Enter the Servant.

SERVANT.

    One of the ships is new come from the Islands;
    The greatest man of note's one Captain Goodlack.
    It is but a small vessel.

Enter Goodlack *and* Sailors.

GOODLACK.

    I'll meet you straight at th' Windmill.
    Not one word of my name.

1 SAILOR.   We understand you.   20
                                   [*Exeunt* Sailors.]

MAYOR.

    Sir, 'tis told us you came late from th'Islands.

GOODLACK.

    I did so.

MAYOR.

    Pray, sir, the news from thence?

GOODLACK.

    The best is that the general is in health
    And Fayal won from th' Spaniards, but the fleet   25
    By reason of so many dangerous tempests

---

    8. *state*] situation (ownership of the tavern, because it is so prosperous).
    9. *a brace*] a pair, two.
    14. *stretch . . . purse*] pay a large dowry.
    15. *motion*] purpose.

Extremely weather-beaten. You, sir, I take it,
Are mayor o'th' town.

MAYOR.   I am the queen's lieutenant.

GOODLACK.

I have some letters of import from one,
A gentleman of very good account   30
That died late in the Islands, to a maid
That keeps a tavern here.

MAYOR.   Her name Bess Bridges?

GOODLACK.

The same. I was desir'd to make inquiry
What fame she bears and what report she's of.
Now you, sir, being here chief magistrate,   35
Can best resolve me.

MAYOR.   To our understanding
She's without stain or blemish well reputed,
And by her modesty and fair demeanor
Hath won the love of all.

GOODLACK [aside].   The worse for me.

ALDERMAN.

I can assure you, many narrow eyes   40
Have look'd on her and her condition,
But those that with most envy have endeavor'd
T'entrap her have return'd won by her virtues.

GOODLACK.

So all that I inquire of make report.
I am glad to hear't. Sir, I have now some business,   45
And I of force must leave you.

MAYOR.   I entreat you
To sup with me tonight.

GOODLACK.   Sir, I may trouble you.
                    [Exeunt Mayor, Alderman, and Servant.]
Five hundred pound a year out of my way.
Is there no flaw that I can tax her with
To forfeit this revenue? Is she such a saint   50
None can missay her? Why then I myself
Will undertake it. If in her demeanor

28. queen's] this edn.; Kings Q.

40. narrow] closely observing, prying.

-49-

I can but find one blemish, stain, or spot,
It is five hundred pound a year well got.   *Exit.*

[III.iii]
Enter Clem *and the* Sailors *on the one side; at the other,* Roughman, *who draws upon them and beats them off.*

Enter Bess, Clem, *and the* Sailors.

BESS.

But did he fight it bravely?

CLEM.

I assure you, mistress, most dissolutely; he hath run this
sailor three times through the body and yet never touch'd
his skin.

BESS.

How can that be?   5

CLEM.

Through the body of his doublet I meant.

BESS.

How shame, base imputation, and disgrace
Can make a coward valiant! Sirrah, you
Look to the bar.

CLEM.

I'll hold up my hand there presently.   [*Exit.*]   10

BESS.

I understand you came now from the Islands.

1 SAILOR.

We did so.

BESS.

If you can tell me tidings of one gentleman,
I shall requite you largely.

1 SAILOR.   Of what name?

BESS.

One Spencer.

2 SAILOR.   We both saw and knew the man.   15

---

2. *dissolutely*] his mistake for "resolutely."
10. *hold . . . hand*] (1) gain the upper hand, take charge (?); (2) possibly
with allusion to a "man of his hands," a courageous man: i.e., "I too can be
valiant—behind the bar."

BESS.

Only for that call for what wine you please.
Pray tell me where you left him.

2 SAILOR.   In Fayal.

BESS.

Was he in health? How did he fare?

2 SAILOR.   Why, well.

BESS.

For that good news spend, revel, and carouse;
Your reck'ning's paid beforehand. I'm ecstasied,   20
And my delight's unbounded.

1 SAILOR.   Did you love him?

BESS.

Next to my hopes in heaven.

1 SAILOR.   Then change your mirth.

BESS.

Why, as I take it, you told me he was well,
And shall I not rejoice?

1 SAILOR.

He's well in heaven, for, mistress, he is dead.   25

BESS.

Hah, dead! Was't so you said? Th' hast given me, friend,
But one wound yet; speak but that word again
And kill me outright.

2 SAILOR.   He lives not.

BESS.

And shall I? Wilt thou not break, heart?
Are these my ribs wrought out of brass or steel,   30
Thou canst not craze their bars?

1 SAILOR.   Mistress, use patience,
Which conquers all despair.

BESS.   You advise well.
I did but jest with sorrow; you may see
I am now in gentle temper.

2 SAILOR.   True, we see't.

BESS.

Pray take the best room in the house, and there   35
Call for what wine best tastes you. At my leisure

---

31. *craze*] shatter.

I'll visit you myself.

1 SAILOR.   I'll use your kindness.   *Exeunt* [Sailors].

BESS.

That it should be my fate. Poor, poor sweetheart!
I do but think how thou becom'st thy grave,
In which would I lay by thee. What's my wealth   40
To enjoy't without my Spencer? I will now
Study to die that I may live with him.

Enter Goodlack.

GOODLACK [*aside*].

The further I inquire, the more I hear
To my discomfort. If my discontinuance
And change at sea disguise me from her knowledge,   45
I shall have scope enough to prove her fully.
This sadness argues she hath heard some news
Of my friend's death.

BESS.   It cannot, sure, be true
That he is dead; death could not be so envious
To snatch him in his prime. I study to forget   50
That e'er was such a man.

GOODLACK [*aside*].   If not impeach her,
My purpose is to seek to marry her.
If she deny me, I'll conceal the will
Or at the least make her compound for half.—
Save you, fair gentlewoman.

BESS.   You are welcome, sir.   55

GOODLACK.

I hear say there's a whore here that draws wine.
I am sharp set and newly come from sea,
And I would see the trash.

BESS.   Sure, you mistake, sir.
If you desire attendance and some wine,
I can command you both. —Where be these boys?   60

GOODLACK.

Are you the mistress?

---

44. *discontinuance*] absence.
57. *sharp set*] hungry for sex.
58. *trash*] whore.

BESS.   I command the house.

GOODLACK.
     Of what birth are you, pra'y?

BESS.   A tanner's daughter.

GOODLACK.
     Where born?

BESS.   In Somersetshire.

GOODLACK.
     A trade-fall'n tanner's daughter go so brave?
     Oh, you have tricks to compass these gay clothes.   65

BESS.
     None, sir, but what are honest.

GOODLACK.   What's your name?

BESS.
     Bess Bridges most men call me.

GOODLACK.   Y'are a whore.

BESS.
     Sir, I will fetch you wine to wash your mouth;
     It is so foul I fear't may fester else.
     There may be danger in't.   70

GOODLACK [aside].
     Not all this move her patience?

BESS.
     Good sir, at this time I am scarce myself
     By reason of a great and weighty loss
     That troubles me. But I should know that ring.

GOODLACK.
     How, this, you baggage? It was never made   75
     To grace a strumpet's finger.

BESS.
     Pardon, sir; I both must and will leave you.   *Exit.*

GOODLACK.
     Did not this well? This will stick in my stomach.
     I could repent my wrongs done to this maid.
     But I'll not leave her thus; if she still love him,   80
     I'll break her heartstrings with some false report
     Of his unkindness.

---

62. *pra'y*] I pray ye.   65. *to compass*] to obtain by craft.
70. *There . . . in't*] You may catch some disease from it.

Enter Clem.

CLEM.

You are welcome, gentleman. What wine will you drink?
Claret, metheglin, or muscadine? Cider or perry to make
you merry? Aragoosa or peter-see-me, canary or charnico?   85
But by your nose, sir, you should love a cup of malmsey; you
shall have a cup of the best in Cornwall.

GOODLACK.

Here's a brave drawer will quarrel with his wine.

CLEM.

But if you prefer the Frenchman before the Spaniard, you
shall have either here of the deep red grape or the pallid   90
white. You are a pretty tall gentleman; you should love high
country wine: none but clerks and sextons love Graves
wine. Or are you a married man, I'll furnish you with bastard, white or brown according to the complexion of your
bedfellow.   95

GOODLACK.

You rogue, how many years of your prenticeship have you
spent in studying this set speech?

CLEM.

The first line of my part was "Anon, anon, sir," and the first
question I answered to was "loggerhead," or "blockhead,"
I know not whether.   100

84–94. *Claret . . . brown*] *claret,* a yellowish or light red wine; *metheglin,*
spiced mead (usually associated with Wales); *muscadine,* a golden, sweet
wine (muscatel); *perry,* fermented juice of pears, as *cider* is fermented juice of
apples; *Aragoosa,* possibly "Saragossa," which produced common wine
(Verity), which Clem may be conflating with "Aragon" (Bates); *peter-see-
me,* a Spanish wine (corrupted from "Pedro Ximenes," who introduced the
grape bearing his name); *canary,* a sweet white wine from the Canary Islands;
charnico, a wine "said to derive its name from a village near Lisbon, where
the grape was grown" (Bates); *malmsey,* a sweet wine usually from Greece or
Madeira (strong enough to give rise to "malmsey-face," the drunkard's
flush, to which Clem alludes); *Graves wine,* white or red, from the Graves
district near Bordeaux (as at I.ii.64, but here with plays on "burial places,"
which clerks and sextons love, and "buried, low," in contrast with *high
country*); *bastard, white or brown,* a sweet Spanish wine or sweetened wine of
any sort, usually of inferior quality (whose name invited innumerable puns,
all about as poor as this one).

88. *quarrel*] (1) quibble; (2) contend, the sense arising from *brave.*

99. *loggerhead*] stupid person.

GOODLACK.

Speak, where's your mistress?

CLEM.

Gone up to her chamber.

GOODLACK.

Set a pottle of sack in th' fire, and carry it into the next
room.   *Exit.*

CLEM.

Score a pottle of sack in the Crown, and see at the bar for 105
some rotten eggs to burn it. We must have one trick or other
to vent away our bad commodities.   *Exit.*

[III.iv]   *Enter* Bess *with* Spencer's *picture.*

BESS.

To die and not vouchsafe some few commends
Before his death was most unkindly done.
This picture is more courteous. 'Twill not shrink
For twenty thousand kisses; no, nor blush.
Then thou shalt be my husband, and I vow   5
Never to marry other.

                    Enter Goodlack.

GOODLACK.   Where's this harlot?

BESS.

You are immodest, sir, to press thus rudely

Into my private chamber.

GOODLACK.   Pox of modesty
When punks must have it mincing in their mouths!
And have I found thee? Then shalt hence with me.   10
                                                   [*Takes picture.*]

---

106. *rotten . . . it*] Clem is referring to mulled sack: wine, sugar, spices,
beaten yolks of eggs, etc., heated. Cf. *The Merry Wives of Windsor*, III.v.29–33:
"*Falstaff.* . . . Go brew me a pottle of sack finely. *Bardolph.* With eggs, sir?
Falstaff. Simple of itself [i.e., straight]. I'll no pullet sperm in my brewage."
Rotten eggs can be used in cooking without absolutely disastrous results.

107. *vent away*] get rid of.
[III.iv]
9. *punks*] harlots.

BESS.

> Rob me not of the chiefest wealth I have.
> Search all my trunks; take the best jewels there.
> Deprive me not that treasure; I'll redeem it
> With plate and all the little coin I have,
> So I may keep that still.

GOODLACK.   Think'st thou that bribes   15

> Can make me leave my friend's will unperform'd?

BESS.

> What was that friend?

GOODLACK.   One Spencer, dead i'th' Islands,

> Whose very last words uttered at his death
> Were these: "If ever thou shalt come to Foy,
> Take thence my picture and deface it quite,   20
> For let it not be said my portraiture
> Shall grace a strumpet's chamber."

BESS.   'Twas not so!

> You lie; you are a villain! 'Twas not so!
> 'Tis more than sin thus to belie the dead.
> He knew if ever I would have transgress'd   25
> 'T had been with him; he durst have sworn me chaste
> And died in that belief.

GOODLACK.   Are you so brief?

> Nay, I'll not trouble you. God b'oy you.

BESS.

> Yet leave me still that picture, and I'll swear
> You are a gentleman and cannot lie.   30

GOODLACK.

> I am inexorable.

BESS.   Are you a Christian?

> Have you any name that ever good man gave you?
> 'Twas no saint you were call'd after. What's thy name?

GOODLACK.

> My name is Captain Thomas Good—

15. may] *Shepherd (Dyce's notes);*
make *Q*.

---

28. *God b'oy you*] God be with you.

BESS.

    I can see no good in thee. 'Rase that syllable   35
    Out of thy name.

GOODLACK.   Goodlack's my name.

BESS.

    I cry you mercy, sir. I now remember you;
    You were my Spencer's friend, and I am sorry,
    Because he lov'd you, I have been so harsh:
    For whose sake I entreat, ere you take't hence,   40
    I may but take my leave on't.

GOODLACK.   You'll return it?

BESS.

    As I am chaste, I will.

GOODLACK.   For once I'll trust you.

                              [Gives her the picture.]

BESS.

    Oh thou, the perfect semblance of my love
    And all that's left of him, take one sweet kiss
    As my last farewell. Thou resemblest him   45
    For whose sweet safety I was every morning
    Down on my knees, and with the lark's sweet tunes
    I did begin my prayers; and when sad sleep
    Had charm'd all eyes, when none save the bright stars
    Were up and waking, I remember'd thee.   50
    But all, all to no purpose.

GOODLACK [*aside*].

    Sure, most sure, this cannot be dissembled.

BESS.

    To thee I have been constant in thine absence,
    And when I look'd upon this painted piece,
    Remember'd thy last rules and principles.   55
    For thee I have given alms, visited prisons,
    To gentlemen and passengers lent coin,
    That if they ever had ability
    They might repay't to Spencer; yet for this,
    All this and more, I cannot have so much   60
    As this poor table.

---

61. *table*] picture.

GOODLACK [*aside*].   I should question truth,
    If I should wrong this creature.
BESS [*aside*].   I am resolv'd.—
    See, sir, this picture I restore you back,
    Which since it was his will you should take hence,
    I will not wrong the dead.
GOODLACK.   God be wi' you.   65
BESS.

    One word more.
    Spencer, you say, was so unkind in death?
GOODLACK.

    I tell you true.
BESS.

    I do entreat you even for goodness' sake,
    Since you were one that he entirely lov'd,   70
    If you some few days hence hear me expir'd,
    You will, 'mongst other good men and poor people
    That haply may miss Bess, grace me so much
    As follow me to th' grave. This if you promise,
    You shall not be the least of all my friends   75
    Remember'd in my will. Now, fare you well.
GOODLACK [*aside*].

    Had I a heart of flint or adamant,
    It would relent at this. —My Mistress Bess,
    I have better tidings for you.
BESS.   You will restore
    My picture? Will you?
GOODLACK.   Yes, and more than that: 80
    This ring from my friend's finger, sent to you
    With infinite commends.
BESS.   You change my blood.
GOODLACK.

    These writings are the evidence of lands;
    Five hundred pound a year's bequeath'd to you,
    Of which I here possess you. All is yours.   85
BESS.

    This surplusage of love hath made my loss,

---

77. *adamant*] a substance of extreme hardness.
82. *You . . . blood*] you cause me to go pale.

That was but great before, now infinite.—
[*Aside.*] It may be compass'd; there's in this my purpose
No impossibility.

GOODLACK.   What study you?

BESS [*aside*].

Four thousand pound besides this legacy   90
In jewels, gold, and silver I can make,
And every man discharg'd. I am resolv'd
To be a pattern to all maids hereafter
Of constancy in love.

GOODLACK.

Sweet Mistress Bess, will you command my service?   95
If to succeed your Spencer in his love,
I would expose me wholly to your wishes.

BESS.

Alas, my love sleeps with him in his grave
And cannot thence be waken'd; yet for his sake
I will impart a secret to your trust,   100
Which, saving you, no mortal should partake.

GOODLACK.

Both for his love and yours, command my service.

BESS.

There's a prize
Brought into Falmouth Road, a good tight vessel.
The bottom will but cost eight hundred pound.   105
You shall have money; buy it.

GOODLACK.   To what end?

BESS.

That you shall know hereafter. Furnish her
With all provision needful—spare no cost—
And join with you a ging of lusty lads,
Such as will bravely man her. All the charge   110
I will commit to you; and when she's fitted,
Captain, she is thine own.

GOODLACK.   I sound it not.

---

92. *discharg'd*] paid in full.
105. *bottom*] ship, without cargo.
109. *ging*] gang, or, more specifically, crew of ship.
112. *sound*] understand, fathom.

BESS.

    Spare me the rest. —[*Aside.*]   This voyage I intend;
    Though some may blame, all lovers will commend.   *Exeunt.*

               Explicit Actus tertius.

[IV.i]

After an alarum, enter a Spanish Captain *with* Sailors, *bringing in a* Merchant, Spencer, *and the* Surgeon *prisoners.*

SPANISH CAPTAIN.

    For Fayal's loss, and spoil by th'English done,
    We are in part reveng'd. There's not a vessel
    That bears upon her top St. George's Cross,
    But for that act shall suffer.

MERCHANT.   Insult not, Spaniard,

    Nor be too proud that thou by odds of ships,   5
    Provision, men, and powder mad'st us yield.
    Had you come one to one or made assault
    With reasonable advantage, we by this
    Had made the carcass of your ship your graves,
    Low sunk to the sea's bottom.   10

SPANISH CAPTAIN.

    Englishman, thy ship shall yield us pillage.
    These prisoners we will keep in strongest hold,
    To pay no other ransom than their lives.

SPENCER.

    Degenerate Spaniard, there's no noblesse in thee,
    To threaten men unarm'd and miserable.   15
    Thou might'st as well tread o'er a field of slaughter
    And kill them o'er that are already slain,
    And brag thy manhood.

SPANISH CAPTAIN.   Sirrah, what are you?

SPENCER.

    Thy equal as I am a prisoner,
    But once today a better man than thou,   20
    A gentleman in my country.

20. today] *Brereton*; to stay *Q*.

SPANISH CAPTAIN.

    Wert thou not so, we have strappados, bolts,

    And engines to the mainmast fastened,

    Can make you gentle.

SPENCER.   Spaniard, do thy worst.

    Thou canst not act more tortures than my courage   25

    Is able to endure.

SPANISH CAPTAIN.   These Englishmen!

    Nothing can daunt them. Even in misery

    They'll not regard their masters.

SPENCER.

    Masters! Insulting, bragging Thrasos!

SPANISH CAPTAIN.

    His sauciness we'll punish 'bove the rest.   30

    About their censures we will next devise—   *Flourish.*

    And now towards Spain with our brave English prize.   *Exeunt.*

[IV.ii]   *Enter* Bess, Mayor, Alderman, Clem.

BESS.

    A table and some stools!

                            A table set out, and stools.

CLEM.

    I shall give you occasion to ease your tails presently.

BESS.

    Will't please you sit?

MAYOR.   With all our hearts, and thank you.

BESS.

    Fetch me that parchment in my closet window.

   22–23. *strappados . . . engines*] instruments of torture or restraint. In the *strappado* the victim was raised aloft by means of a line fastened to his hands crossed in back, then dropped and halted with a jerk; *bolts* were fetters or shackles; *engines* was used generally to mean "devices" or specifically to mean "racks."

   29. *Thrasos*] braggarts (Thraso is the braggart warrior in Terence's *Eunuchus*).

   31. *censures*] sentences.

[IV.ii]

   4. *closet*] sitting-room.

CLEM.

    The three sheepskins with the wrong side outward?   5

BESS.

    That with the seal.

CLEM [*aside*].

    I hope it is my indenture, and now she means to give me my
    time.   [*Exit.*]

ALDERMAN.

    And now you are alone, fair Mistress Elzabeth,
    I think it good to taste you with a motion   10
    That no way can displease you.

BESS.   Pray, speak on.

ALDERMAN.

    'T hath pleas'd here Master Mayor so far to look
    Into your fair demeanor that he thinks you
    A fit match for his son.

Enter Clem *with the parchment.*

CLEM.

    Here's the parchment, but if it be the lease of your house, I   15
    can assure you 'tis out.

BESS.

    The years are not expired.

CLEM.

    No, but it is out of your closet.

BESS.

    About your business.

CLEM.

    Here's even Susanna betwixt the two wicked elders.   [*Exit.*]   20

ALDERMAN.

    What think you, Mistress Elzabeth?

---

    10. *taste*] try, see whether it is to your taste.
    16. *'tis out*] has expired.
    20. *Susanna*] According to the *Apocrypha*, the chaste and beautiful
Susanna resisted the advances of two lustful elders and was for revenge
accused of adultery by them. Their falsehood was exposed by Daniel.
Susanna and the Elders were frequent subjects of Elizabethan tapestries and
paintings.

BESS.   Sir, I thank you;
   And how much I esteem this goodness from you
   The trust I shall commit unto your charge
   Will truly witness. Marry, gentle sir!
   'Las, I have sadder business now in hand   25
   Than sprightly marriage; witness these my tears.
   Pray read these.
MAYOR [*reads*].
   "The last will and testament of Elzabeth Bridges, to be
   committed to the trust of the Mayor and Aldermen of Foy
   and their successors forever: 30
      To set up young beginners in their trade, a thousand
      pound.
      To relieve such as have had loss by sea, five hundred
      pound.
      To every maid that's married out of Foy whose name's   35
      Elzabeth, ten pound.
      To relieve maimed soldiers, by the year ten pound.
      To Captain Goodlack, if he shall perform the business he's
      employed in, five hundred pound.
   "The legacies for Spencer thus to stand: 40
      To number all the poorest of his kin and to bestow on
      them, Item, to——"
BESS.
   Enough. You see, sir, I am now too poor
   To bring a dowry with me fit for your son.
MAYOR.
   You want a precedent, you so abound   45
   In charity and goodness.
BESS.   All my servants
   I leave at your discretions to dispose.
   Not one but I have left some legacy.
   What shall become of me, or what I purpose,
   Spare further to inquire.
MAYOR.   We'll take our leaves   50
   And prove to you faithful executors
   In this bequest.
ALDERMAN.   Let never such despair,
  As, dying rich, shall make the poor their heir.

                                 Exit [*with* Mayor].

BESS.

Why, what is all the wealth the world contains,
Without my Spencer?

Enter Roughman *and* Forset.

ROUGHMAN.   Where's my sweet Bess?   55
Shall I become a welcome suitor now
That I have chang'd my copy?
BESS.   I joy to hear it.
I'll find employment for you.

Enter Goodlack, Sailors, *and* Clem.

GOODLACK.

A gallant ship and wondrous proudly trimm'd;
Well caulk'd, well tackled, every way prepar'd.   60
BESS.

Here then our mourning for a season end.
ROUGHMAN.

Bess, shall I strike that captain? Say the word,
I'll have him by the ears.
BESS.   Not for the world.
GOODLACK.

What saith that fellow?
BESS.   He desires your love;
Good Captain, let him ha' it.
GOODLACK.   Then change a hand.   65
BESS.

Resolve me all. I am bound upon a voyage.
Will you in this adventure take such part
As I myself shall do?
ROUGHMAN.

With my fair Bess, to the world's end.
BESS.

Then, Captain and Lieutenant both join hands;   70
Such are your places now.
GOODLACK.   We two are friends.
BESS.

I next must swear you two, with all your ging,

57. *chang'd my copy*] altered my character.
66. *Resolve me all*] everyone assure me.

-64-

True to some articles you must observe,
Reserving to myself a prime command
Whilst I enjoin nothing unreasonable.   75

GOODLACK.

All this is granted.

BESS.

Then first, you said your ship was trim and gay;
I'll have her pitch'd all o'er: no spot of white,
No color to be seen, no sail but black,
No flag but sable.

GOODLACK.   'Twill be ominous   80
And bode disaster fortune.

BESS.   I'll ha't so.

GOODLACK.

Why then she shall be pitch'd black as the devil.

BESS.

She shall be call'd the *Negro*. When you know
My conceit, Captain, you will thank me for't.

ROUGHMAN.

But whither are we bound?

BESS.   Pardon me that;   85
When we are out at sea, I'll tell you all.
For mine own wearing I have rich apparel,
For man or woman as occasion serves.

CLEM.

But, mistress, if you be going to sea, what shall become of me
a-land?   90

BESS.

I'll give thee thy full time.

CLEM.

And shall I take time, when time is, and let my mistress slip
away? No, it shall be seen that my teeth are as strong to
grind biscuit as the best sailor of them all, and my stomach
as able to digest powder'd beef and poor-john. Shall I stay   95
here to score a pudding in the Half-moon, and see my mistress

84. me] *Collier*; *not in Q.*

_____

84. *conceit*] idea.
92. *take time, when time*] loiter, when opportunity.
95. *powder'd*] salted.
95. *poor-john*] salted fish.

at the mainyard, with her sails up and spread? No, it shall
be seen that I, who have been brought up to draw wine, will
see what water the ship draws, or I'll bewray the voyage.

BESS.

If thou hast so much courage, the captain shall accept thee.   100

CLEM.

If I have so much courage? When did you see a black
beard with a white liver or a little fellow without a tall
stomach? I doubt not but to prove an honor to all the
drawers in Cornwall.

GOODLACK.

What now remains?

FORSET.   To make myself associate   105
In this bold enterprise.

GOODLACK.   Most gladly, sir.
And now our number's full, what's to be done?

BESS.

First, at my charge I'll feast the town of Foy;
Then set the cellars ope, that these my mates
May quaff unto the health of our boon voyage.   110
Our needful things being once convey'd aboard,
Then, casting up our caps in sign of joy,
Our purpose is to bid farewell to Foy.   [*Exeunt.*]

Hautboys long.

---

99. *bewray*] expose, perhaps with pun on "beray," befoul, from the idea of
drawing water.

101–102. *black beard*] Clem seems extraordinarily precocious. Perhaps
Heywood has forgotten that he is newly come into his teens (II.i.30), or
perhaps there is supposed to be a ludicrous contrast between his words and
his appearance.

102. *white liver*] a sign of cowardice, the liver being the seat of courage.

102–103. *tall stomach*] appetite for glory.

110. *boon voyage*] good success (*bon voyage*).

113.1. *Hautboys long*] This notation and *Act long* at IV.v.19.1 probably
indicate that Heywood anticipated the use of elaborate props in the
representation of the court of Fez. These presumably would require extra
time for arrangement.

[IV.iii]

Enter Mullisheg, Bashaw Alcade, *and* Joffer, *with other attendants.*

MULLISHEG.

    Out of these bloody and intestine broils,
    We have at length attain'd a fort'nate peace,
    And now at last establish'd in the throne
    Of our great ancestors, and reign King
    Of Fez and great Morocco.

ALCADE.   Mighty Mullisheg,   5

    Pride of our age and glory of the Moors,
    By whose victorious hand all Barbary
    Is conquer'd, aw'd, and sway'd, behold thy vassals
    With loud applauses greet thy victory.   *Shout. Flourish.*

MULLISHEG.

    Upon the slaughtered bodies of our foes,   10
    We mount our high tribunal, and being sole,
    Without competitor, we now have leisure
    To 'stablish laws, first for our kingdom's safety,
    The enriching of our public treasury,
    And last our state and pleasure. Then give order   15
    That all such Christian merchants as have traffic
    And freedom in our country, that conceal
    The least part of our custom due to us,
    Shall forfeit ship and goods.

JOFFER.   There are appointed
    Unto that purpose careful officers.   20

MULLISHEG.

    Those forfeitures must help to furnish up
    Th'exhausted treasure that our wars consum'd.
    Part of such profits as accrue that way
    We have already tasted.

    0.1. *Mullisheg . . . Joffer*] Alcade, which Heywood uses as a given name, is
actually a title. ". . . Muleis, are the Kings children, and all other who are
of the blood royal, are termed by this name. . . . Bashas, are Captaine
Generalls over armies. . . . Alkeids be the Lords, set aswell over Garrison
Townes as Countreys, to rule and keep the people in subjection" (RO.C.,
A True Historical Discourse of Muly Hamet's Rising [1609]). Heywood seems at
least vaguely to have understood the significance of the titles.
    18. *custom*] duties, tariffs.

ALCADE.   'Tis most fit
    Those Christians that reap profit by our land   25
    Should contribute unto so great a loss.

MULLISHEG.
    Alcade, they shall. But what's the style of king
    Without his pleasure? Find us concubines,
    The fairest Christian damsels you can hire
    Or buy for gold, the loveliest of the Moors   30
    We can command, and Negroes everywhere.
    Italians, French, and Dutch, choice Turkish girls
    Must fill our Alkedavy, the great palace
    Where Mullisheg now deigns to keep his court.

JOFFER.
    Who else are worthy to be libertines   35
    But such as bear the sword?

MULLISHEG.   Joffer, thou pleasest us.
    If kings on earth be termed demigods,
    Why should we not make here terrestrial heaven?
    We can, we will; our god shall be our pleasure,
    For so our Meccan prophet warrants us.   40
    And now the music of the drums surcease;
    We'll learn to dance to the soft tunes of peace.

Hautboys. [Exeunt.]

[IV.iv]   *Enter* Bess *like a sea captain*, Goodlack, [*and*] Roughman.

BESS.
    Good morrow, Captain. Oh, this last sea fight
    Was gallantly perform'd! It did me good
    To see the Spanish carvel vail her top
    Unto my maiden flag. Where ride we now?

35–36. JOFFER. Who . . . thou] *Q* (*c*);   0.1. Roughman.] *Verity* (Roughman,
Mull. Ioffer. Who . . . *Ioff.* Thou   *and others*); *Roughman, Forset, and*
Q (*u*).   *Clem. Q.*

---

   33. *Alkedavy*] as Heywood says, the "great palace," but at V.ii.107 spoken
of as though it were an interior part of the palace, unless we are to imagine
V.ii as being located in some public place.
[IV.iv]
   3. *carvel*] small, fast ship.
   3. *vail her top*] lower her topsail (signifying surrender).

GOODLACK.

    Among the Islands.   5

BESS.

    What coast is this we now descry from far?

GOODLACK.

    Yon fort's call'd Fayal.

BESS.

    Is that the place where Spencer's body lies?

GOODLACK.

    Yes, in yon church he's buried.

BESS.

    Then know to this place was my voyage bound   10
    To fetch the body of my Spencer thence,
    In his own country to erect a tomb
    And lasting monument, where when I die
    In the same bed of earth my bones may lie.
    Then all that love me, arm and make for shore.   15
    Yours be the spoil, he mine; I crave no more.

ROUGHMAN.

    May that man die derided and accurs'd
    That will not follow where a woman leads.

GOODLACK.

    Roughman, you are too rash and counsel ill.
    Have not the Spaniards fortified the town?   20
    In all our ging we are but sixty-five.

ROUGHMAN.

    Come, I'll make one.

GOODLACK.   Attend me, good Lieutenant;
    And, sweet Bess, listen what I have devis'd.
    With ten tall fellows I have mann'd our boat
    To see what straggling Spaniards they can take.   25
    And see where Forset is return'd with prisoners.

Enter Forset *with two* Spaniards.

FORSET.

    These Spaniards we by break of day surpris'd
    As they were ready to take boat for fishing.

---

6. *descry*] discover.

GOODLACK.

    Spaniards, upon your lives resolve us truly,

    How strong's the town and fort?   30

1 SPANIARD.

    Since English Raleigh won and spoil'd it first,

    The town's re-edified and fort new built,

    And four field pieces in the blockhouse lie

    To keep the harbor's mouth.

GOODLACK.

    And what's one ship to these?   35

BESS.

    Was there not in the time of their abode

    A gentleman call'd Spencer buried there

    Within the church, whom some report was slain

    Or perish'd by a wound?

1 SPANIARD.   Indeed there was

    And o'er him rais'd a goodly monument,   40

    But when the English navy were sail'd thence

    And that the Spaniards did possess the town,

    Because they held him for an heretic,

    They straight remov'd his body from the church.

BESS.

    And would the tyrants be so uncharitable   45

    To wrong the dead? Where did they then bestow him?

1 SPANIARD.

    They buried him i'th' fields.

BESS.   Oh, still more cruel!

1 SPANIARD.

    The man that ought the field, doubtful his corn

    Would never prosper whilst an heretic's body

    Lay there, he made petition to the Church   50

    To ha' it digg'd up and burnt, and so it was.

BESS.

    What's he that loves me would persuade me live,

    Not rather leap o'er hatches into th' sea?

    Yet ere I die, I hope to be reveng'd

    Upon some Spaniards for my Spencer's wrong.   55

---

48. *ought*] owned.

ROUGHMAN.

    Let's first begin with these.

BESS.

    'Las, these poor slaves! Besides their pardon'd lives,
    One give them money. —And, Spaniards, where you come,
    Pray for Bess Bridges, and speak well o'th' English.

SPANIARDS.

    We shall.   60

BESS.

    Our mourning we will turn into revenge.
    And since the Church hath censur'd so my Spencer,
    Bestow upon the Church some few cast pieces.—
    Command the gunner do't.

GOODLACK.

    And if he can to batter it to the earth   *A piece.*   65

             Enter Clem *falling for haste.*

CLEM.

    A sail, a sail!

BESS.

    From whence?

CLEM.

    A pox upon yon gunner! Could he not give warning before
    he had shot?

ROUGHMAN.

    Why, I prithee?   70

CLEM.

    Why? I was sent to the top-mast to watch, and there I fell
    fast asleep. "Bounce," quoth the guns; down tumbles Clem,
    and if by chance my feet had not hung in the tackles, you
    must have sent to England for a bone-setter, for my neck had
    been in a pitiful taking.   75

ROUGHMAN.

    Thou told'st us of a sail.

60. S.P. SPANIARDS] *Verity*; *Span.* Q.

---

    63. *pieces*] cannon, which are *cast* in metal for the purpose of *casting*
projectiles, which in this instance will be *cast-off* upon the Church.
    65. S.D. *A piece*] A cannon is fired.

Enter Sailor *above.*

SAILOR.

> Arm, gentlemen! A gallant ship of war
> Makes with her full sails this way, who it seems
> Hath took a bark of England.

BESS.   Which we'll rescue

> Or perish in th'adventure. You have sworn   80
> That howsoe'er we conquer or miscarry
> Not to reveal my sex.

ALL.

> We have.

BESS.

> Then, for your country's honor, my revenge,
> For your own fame and hope of golden spoil,   85
> Stand bravely to't. —[*To* Goodlack.]   The manage of the fight
> We leave to you.

GOODLACK.

> Then, now up with your fights, and let your ensigns,
> Blest with St. George's Cross, play with the winds.—
> Fair Bess, keep you your cabin.   90

BESS.

> Captain, you wrong me. I will face the fight,
> And where the bullets sing loud'st 'bout mine ears,
> There shall you find me cheering up my men.

ROUGHMAN.

> This wench would of a coward make an Hercules.

BESS.

> Trumpets, a charge; and with your whistles shrill,   95
> Sound, boatswains, an alarum to your mates!
> With music cheer up their astonish'd souls,
> The whilst the thund'ring ordnance bear the bass.

GOODLACK.

> To fight against the Spaniards we desire.
> Alarum, trumpets!   *Alarum.*

ROUGHMAN.   Gunners, straight give fire!   *Shot.* 100
>   [*Excursions.*]

---

88. *fights*] protective screens.

97. *astonish'd*] shocked, dismayed.

100.1, 105.1. *Excursions*] The characters dash off, their absence being covered by battle noises. The brief clearing of the stage does not mark a new scene.

Enter Goodlack *hurt*, Bess, Roughman, Forset, Clem.

GOODLACK.

    I am shot and can no longer man the deck,

    Yet let not my wound daunt your courage, mates.

BESS.

    For every drop of blood that thou hast shed,

    I'll have a Spaniard's life. —Advance your targets,

    And now cry all, "Board, board! Amain for England!"   105

                                           Alarum.

                          [*Excursions. Exit* Goodlack.]

Enter with victory Bess, Roughman, Forset, Clem, *&c. The Spaniards* [*and their* Captain] *prisoners.*

BESS.

    How is it with the captain?

ROUGHMAN.   Nothing dangerous,

    But being shot i'th' thigh he keeps his cabin

    And cannot rise to greet your victory.

BESS.

    He stood it bravely out whilst he could stand.

CLEM.

    But for these Spaniards—now, you Don Diegos, you that   110

    made Paul's to stink—

ROUGHMAN.

    Before we further censure them, let's know

    What English prisoners they have here aboard.   [*Exit.*]

SPANISH CAPTAIN.

    You may command them all. We that were now

    Lords over them, fortune hath made your slaves.—   115

    Release our prisoners.

BESS.   Had my captain died,

---

    109. *stood it . . . out*] resisted.

    110–111. *you Don . . . stink*] A story about a Spaniard who disgraced
himself in Saint Paul's Cathedral seems to have been current about 1600: it
is alluded to in *Sir Thomas Wyatt*, IV.ii.56–57 (written 1602–1607); *The
Captain*, III. ii (1609–1612, where the Spaniard is "old Don Diego"); and
Blurt, Master Constable, IV.iii.135 (1601–1602); as well as in a rather nasty
letter written in the autumn of 1596 evidently by Nash to a William Cotton
(Ronald B. McKerrow, ed., *The Works of Thomas Nashe*, V, 195).

Not one proud Spaniard had escap'd with life.
Your ship is forfeit to us and your goods,
So live. —Give him his long boat; him and his
Set safe ashore. —And pray for English Bess.   120

SPANISH CAPTAIN.

I know not whom you mean, but be't your queen,
Famous Elizabeth, I shall report
She and her subjects both are merciful.

Exeunt [Captain *and Spaniards*].

Enter Roughman, *with the* [English] Merchant *and* Spencer.

BESS.

Whence are you, sir, and whither were you bound?

MERCHANT.

I am a' London, bound for Barbary,   125
But by this Spanish man-of-war surpris'd,
Pillag'd, and captiv'd.

BESS.   We much pity you.
What loss you have sustain'd, this Spanish prey
Shall make good to you to the. utmost farthing.

MERCHANT.

Our lives and all our fortunes whatsoever   130
Are wholly at your service.

BESS.

These gentlemen have been dejected long.
Let me peruse them all and give them money
To drink our health. And pray forget not, sirs,
To pray for— [*She sees* Spencer.]   Hold, support me or I   135
faint.

ROUGHMAN.

What sudden unexpected ecstasy
Disturbs your conquest?

BESS.   Interrupt me not,
But give me way for heaven's sake!

SPENCER.   I have seen
A face ere now like that young gentleman,
But not remember where.

---

133. *peruse*] inspect.
136. *ecstasy*] swoon, state of shock.

BESS.   But he was slain,   140
    Lay buried in yon church, and thence remov'd,
    Denied all Christian rites, and, like an infidel,
    Confin'd unto the fields; and thence digg'd up.
    His body after death had martyrdom.
    All these assure me 'tis his shadow dogs me,   145
    For some most just revenge, thus far to sea.—
    Is it because the Spaniards 'scap'd with life,
    That were to thee so cruel after death,
    Thou haunt'st me thus? Sweet ghost, thy rage forbear;
    I will revenge thee on the next we seize.—   150
    I am amaz'd; this sight I'll not endure.—
    Sleep, sleep, fair ghost, for thy revenge is sure.
ROUGHMAN.
    Forset, convey the owner to his cabin.   [*Exit* Forset *with* Bess.]
SPENCER.
    I pray, sir, what young gentleman is that?
ROUGHMAN.
    He's both the owner of the ship and goods,   155
    That for some reasons hath his name conceal'd.
SPENCER [*aside*].
    Methink he looks like Bess, for in his eyes
    Lives the first love that did my heart surprise.
ROUGHMAN.
    Come, gentlemen, first make your losses good
    Out of this Spanish prize. Let's then divide   160
    Both several ways, and heavens be our guide.
MERCHANT.
    We towards Mamorah.
ROUGHMAN.   We where the Fates do please,
    Till we have track'd a wilderness of seas.   [*Exeunt.*]

[IV.v]   *Flourish. Enter* Chorus.

CHORUS.
    Our stage so lamely can express a sea
    That we are forc'd by Chorus to discourse
    What should have been in action. Now imagine
    Her passion o'er and Goodlack well recover'd,
    Who, had he not been wounded and seen Spencer,   5

Had sure descried him. Much prize they have ta'en.
The French and Dutch she spares, only makes spoil
Of the rich Spaniard and the barbarous Turk,
And now her fame grows great in all these seas.
Suppose her rich, and forc'd for want of water   10
To put into Mamorah in Barbary,
Where, wearied with the habit of a man,
She was discover'd by the Moors aboard,
Which told it to the amorous King of Fez,
That ne'er before had English lady seen.   15
He sends for her on shore. How he receives her,
How she and Spencer meet must next succeed.
Sit patient then. When these are fully told,
Some may hap say, "Ay, there's a girl worth gold."   *Exit.*

Act long.

Explicit Actus quartus.

[V.i]   *Enter* Mullisheg, Alcade, Joffer, *and attendants, &c.*

MULLISHEG.
     But was she of such presence?
ALCADE.   To describe her
     Were to make eloquence dumb.
MULLISHEG.   Well habited?
ALCADE.
     I ne'er beheld a beauty more complete.
MULLISHEG.
     Thou hast inflam'd our spirits. In England born?
ALCADE.
     The captain so reported.
MULLISHEG.   How her ship?   5
ALCADE.
     I never saw a braver vessel sail,
     And she is call'd the *Negro.*
MULLISHEG.   Ominous

19. S.D. *Exit*] *Collier*; *Exeunt* Q.

---

12. *habit*] costume.
19.1. *Act long*] indicating a longer interval than usual between the acts
(cf. IV.ii.113.1 and note).

Perhaps to our good fate; she in a *Negro*
Hath sail'd thus far to bosom with a Moor.
But for the motion made to come ashore,   10
How did she relish that?

ALCADE.

I promis'd to the captain large reward
To win him to it, and this day he'ath promis'd
To bring me her free answer.

MULLISHEG.   When he comes,
Give him the entertainment of a prince.   15

Enter a Moor.

The news with thee?

MOOR.

The captain of the *Negro* craves admittance
Unto your highness' presence.

MULLISHEG.

A guard attend him, and our noblest bashaws
Conduct him safe where we will parley him.   *Flourish.*   20

Enter Goodlack *and* Roughman.

GOODLACK.

Long live the high and mighty King of Fez!

MULLISHEG.

If thou bring'st her, then dost thou bring me life.
Say, will she come?

GOODLACK.

She will, my lord, but yet conditionally
She may be free from violence.   25

MULLISHEG.

Now, by the mighty prophet we adore,
She shall live lady of her free desires;
'Tis love, not force, must quench our amorous fires.

ROUGHMAN.

We will conduct her to your presence straight.
                    [*Exeunt* Roughman *and* Goodlack.]

MULLISHEG.

We will have banquets, revels, and what not   30
To entertain this stranger.   *Hautboys.*

Enter Bess Bridges *veil'd*, Goodlack, Roughman, Forset, *and Moors.*

A goodly presence! Why's that beauty veil'd?

BESS.

Long live the King of Fez!   [*Unveils.*]

MULLISHEG.   I am amaz'd!

This is no mortal creature I behold,

But some bright angel that is dropp'd from heaven,   35

Sent by our prophet. —Captain, let me thus

Embrace thee in my arms. —Load him with gold,

For this great favor.

BESS.   Captain, touch it not.—

Know, King of Fez, my followers want no gold.

I only came to see thee for my pleasure   40

And show thee what these say thou never saw'st,

A woman born in England.

MULLISHEG.

That English earth may well be term'd a heaven,

That breeds such divine beauties. Make me sure

That thou art mortal by one friendly touch.   45

BESS.

Keep off; for till thou swear'st to my demands,

I will have no commerce with Mullisheg,

But leave thee as I came.

MULLISHEG.   Were't half my kingdom,

That, beauteous English virgin, thou shalt have.

BESS.

Captain, read.   [*Hands* Goodlack *a paper.*]   50

GOODLACK [*reads*].

"First, liberty for her and hers to leave the land at her pleasure.

Next, safe conduct to and from her ship at her own discretion.

Thirdly, to be free from all violence either by the king or any of his people.   55

Fourthly, to allow her mariners fresh victuals aboard.

Fifthly, to offer no further violence to her person than what he seeks by kindly usage and free entreaty."

58. kindly] *Verity*; kingly *Q*.

47. *commerce*] social intercourse.

MULLISHEG.

    To these I vow and seal.

BESS.   These being assur'd,

    Your courtship's free, and henceforth we secur'd.   60

MULLISHEG.

    Say, gentlemen of England, what's your fashion

    And garb of entertainment?

GOODLACK.   Our first greeting

    Begins still on the lips.

MULLISHEG.

    Fair creature, shall I be immortaliz'd

    With that high favor?

BESS.   'Tis no immodest thing   65

    You ask, nor shame for Bess to kiss a king.   [*Kisses him.*]

MULLISHEG.

    This kiss hath all my vitals ecstasied.

ROUGHMAN [*to* Goodlack].

    Captain,

    This king is mightily in love. Well, let her

    Do as she list, I'll make use of his bounty.   70

GOODLACK [*to him*].

    We should be madmen else.

MULLISHEG.

    Grace me so much as take your seat by me.

BESS.

    I'll be so far commanded.

MULLISHEG.   Sweet, your age?

BESS.

    Not fully yet seventeen.

MULLISHEG.

    But how your birth? How came you to this wealth,   75

    To have such gentlemen at your command,

    And what your cause of travel?

BESS.   Mighty prince,

    If you desire to see me beat my breast,

    Pour forth a river of increasing tears,

    Then you may urge me to that sad discourse.   80

---

62. *garb*] style.
70. *list*] pleases.

MULLISHEG.

    Not for Mamorah's wealth nor all the gold
    Coin'd in rich Barbary. Nay, sweet, arise,
    And ask of me, be't half this kingdom's treasure
    And thou art lady on't.

BESS.

    If I shall ask, 't must be you will not give.   85
    Our country breeds no beggars, for our hearts
    Are of more noble temper.

MULLISHEG.   Sweet, your name.

BESS.

    Elizabeth.

MULLISHEG.   There's virtue in that name.
    The virgin queen, so famous through the world,
    The mighty empress of the maiden isle,   90
    Whose predecessors have o'errun great France,
    Whose powerful hand doth still support the Dutch
    And keeps the potent King of Spain in awe,
    Is not she titled so?

BESS.   She is.

MULLISHEG.

    Hath she herself a face so fair as yours,   95
    When she appears for wonder?

BESS.   Mighty Fez,
    You cast a blush upon my maiden cheek
    To pattern me with her. Why, England's queen,
    She is the only phoenix of her age,
    The pride and glory of the Western Isles.   100
    Had I a thousand tongues, they all would tire
    And fail me in her true description.

MULLISHEG.

    Grant me this:
    Tomorrow we supply our judgment seat
    And sentence causes; sit with us in state,   105

---

    85. *If . . . give*] i.e., in the unlikely event of my asking, you must not give.

    96. *for wonder*] in order to be wondered at.

    98. *pattern*] compare.

    99. *phoenix*] paragon of beauty and excellence (only one phoenix lived at
a time).

    105. *sentence causes*] judge legal cases.

And let your presence beautify our throne.

BESS.

In that I am your servant.

MULLISHEG.   And we thine.
Set on in state, attendants and full train.
But find to ask, we vow thou shalt obtain.

                                        [*Exeunt.*] *Manet* Goodlack.

Enter Clem [*as a fantastic Moor*].

CLEM.

"It is not now as when Andrea liv'd,"—or rather Andrew, 110
our elder journeyman. What, drawers become courtiers?
Now may I speak with the old ghost in *Jeronimo*:
   When this eternal substance of my soul
   Did live imprisoned in this wanton flesh,
   I was a courtier in the court of Fez.   115

GOODLACK.

Oh, well done, Clem! It is your mistress' pleasure,
None come ashore that's not well habited.

CLEM.

Nay, for mine own part, I hold myself as good a Christian in
these clothes as the proudest infidel of them all.

Enter Alcade *and* Joffer.

ALCADE.

Sir, by your leave, y'are of the English train?   120

CLEM.

I am so, thou great monarch of the Mauritanians.

JOFFER.

Then, 'tis the king's command we give you all attendance.

CLEM.

Great Signior of the Saracens, I thank thee.

109.1. *Manet Goodlack*] Goodlack remains.
110–111. *It . . . journeyman*] Clem quotes a scrap of Kyd's *Spanish Tragedy*;
or Hieronimo is Mad Again (IV.vii.111), a favorite old play. The line was
famous: cf. Jonson's *Staple of News* (I.iv.17) and Fletcher's *Woman's Prize*
(II.vi).
113–115. *When . . . Fez*] the opening lines of *The Spanish Tragedy* (approxi-
mately), with "court of Fez" substituted for "the Spanish court."
121. *Mauritanians*] Ancient Mauritania occupied parts of modern Morocco
and western Algeria. Clem is, of course, speaking loosely.

ALCADE.

Will you walk in to banquet?

CLEM.

I will make bold to march in towards your banquet and   125
there comfit myself, and cast all caraways down my throat,
the best way I have to conserve myself in health; and for
your country's sake, which is called Barbary, I will love all
barbers and barberies the better.

> And for you Moors, thus much I mean to say,   130
> I'll see if Moor I eat, the Moor I may.

Enter two Merchants, [French *and* Italian].

FRENCH MERCHANT.

I pray, sir, are you of the English train?

CLEM.

Why, what art thou, my friend?

FRENCH MERCHANT.

Sir, a French merchant run into relapse
And forfeit of the law. Here's for you, sir,   135
Forty good Barbary pieces to deliver
Your lady this petition, who, I hear,
Can all things with the king.

CLEM.

Your gold doth bind me to you. —[*Aside.*] You may see
what it is to be a sudden courtier: I no sooner put my nose 140
into the court, but my hand itches for a bribe already.
—What's your business, my friend?

ITALIAN MERCHANT.

Some of my men for a little outrage done

---

126. *comfit*] help myself to comfits (sweetmeats), from pun on "comfort"
(*OED*).

126. *caraways*] (1) Caraway seeds were used in making confections as well
as in medicines taken to expel flatulence. (2) Quibblingly, "care away."

127. *conserve*] preserve, with allusion to "conserve," a medicine or
confection.

129. *barbers*] (1) inhabitants of Barbery; (2) barber-surgeons.

129. *barberies*] (1) barber shops; (2) barberries, used in cookery and
medicine.

134. *relapse*] failure to pay a claim.

Are sentenc'd to the galleys.

CLEM.

To the gallows?   145

ITALIAN MERCHANT.

No, to the galleys. Now, could your lady purchase
Their pardon from the king, here's twenty angels.

CLEM.

What are you, sir?

ITALIAN MERCHANT.

A Florentine merchant.

CLEM.

Then you are, as they say, a Christian?   150

ITALIAN MERCHANT.

Heaven forbid else.

CLEM.

I should not have the faith to take your gold else.
Attend on me; I'll speak in your behalf.
Where be my bashaws?— Usher us in state,   *Flourish.*
And when we sit to banquet, see you wait.   155
          Exit [Clem *with* Goodlack *and* Merchants, *attended*].

[V.ii]   *Enter* Spencer *solus.*

SPENCER.

This day the king ascends his royal throne.
The honest merchant in whose ship I came
Hath by a cunning quiddit in the law
Both ship and goods made forfeit to the king,
To whom I will petition. But no more;   5
He's now upon his entrance.   *Hautboys.*

Enter the King, Bess, Goodlack, Roughman, Alcade, Joffer, *with all the other train.*

155. sit] *Collier*; fit *Q*.

147. *angels*] gold coins worth about 10*s*. with the image of the archangel
Michael impressed on one face.
[V.ii]
  3. *quiddit*] subtle point.

MULLISHEG.

    Here seat thee, maid of England, like a queen,

    The style we'll give thee, wilt thou deign us love.

BESS.

    Bless me, you holy angels!

MULLISHEG.

    What is't offends you, sweet?   10

SPENCER [aside].

    I am amaz'd and know not what to think on't.

BESS.

    Captain, dost not see? Is not that Spencer's ghost?

                                        [They speak apart.]

GOODLACK.

    I see, and like you I am ecstasied.

SPENCER [aside].

    If mine eyes mistake not,

    That should be Captain Goodlack, and that Bess.   15

    But oh, I cannot be so happy.

GOODLACK.

    'Tis he, and I'll salute him.

BESS.   Captain, stay.

    You shall be sway'd by me.

SPENCER [aside].

    Him I well know, but how should she come hither?

MULLISHEG.

    What is't that troubles you?

BESS.   Most mighty King,   20

    Spare me no longer time but to bestow

    My captain on a message.

MULLISHEG.

    Thou shalt command my silence and his ear.

BESS [to Goodlack].

    Go wind about, and when you see least eyes

    Are fix'd on you, single him out and see   25

    If we mistake not. If he be the man,

    Give me some private note.

---

    17. *salute*] greet.

    21. *bestow*] send.

GOODLACK.

    This.   *[Makes a sign.]*

BESS.

    Enough. —What said your highness?

MULLISHEG.

    Hark what I proffer thee. Continue here,   30

    And grant me full fruition of thy love.

BESS.

    Good.

MULLISHEG.

    Thou shalt have all my peers to honor thee

    Next our great prophet.

BESS.

    Well.   35

MULLISHEG.

    And when th'art weary of our sunburnt clime,

    Thy *Negro* shall be ballast home with gold.

                            [Goodlack *makes the sign.*]

BESS [*aside*].

    I am eterniz'd ever!

    Now, all you sad disasters, dare your worst;

    I neither care nor fear. My Spencer lives!   40

MULLISHEG.

    You mind me not, sweet virgin.

BESS.   You talk of love.

    My lord, I'll tell you more of that hereafter;

    But now to your state business. —[*To* Goodlack.]   Bid him

        do thus

    No more, and not be seen till then.

GOODLACK [*to* Spencer].

    Enough. Come, sir, you must along with me.   45

                    [*Exeunt* Goodlack *and* Spencer.]

BESS [*aside*].

    Now stood a thousand deaths before my face,

    I would not change my cheer since Spencer's safe.

        Enter Clem, [*a* Preacher,] *and the* Merchants.

29. your] *Collier*; you *Q*.

---

38. *eterniz'd*] made immortal.

CLEM.

    By your leave, my masters; room for Generosity.

FRENCH MERCHANT.

    Pray, sir, remember me.

ITALIAN MERCHANT.   Good sir, my suit.

CLEM.

    I am perfect in both your parts without prompting. Mistress,   50
    here are two Christen friends of mine have forfeited ships
    and men to the black-a-morian king. Now one sweet word
    from your lips might get their release. —[*Aside.*] I have
    had a feeling of the business already.

MULLISHEG [*to* French Merchant].

    For dealing in commodities forbid,   55
    Y'are fin'd a thousand ducats.

BESS.

    Cast off the burden of your heavy doom;
    A follower of my train petitions for him.

MULLISHEG.

    One of thy train, sweet Bess?

CLEM.

    And no worse man than myself, sir.   60

MULLISHEG.

    Well, sirrah, for your lady's sake
    His ship and goods shall be restor'd again.

FRENCH MERCHANT.

    Long live the King of Fez!

CLEM.

    May'st thou never want sweet water to wash thy black face
    in, most mighty monarch of Morocco. —Mistress, another   65
    friend. —[*Aside.*] Ay, and paid beforehand.

MULLISHEG.

    Sirrah, your men for outrage and contempt
    Are doom'd unto the galleys.

51. forfeited] *Collier*; forfeiter *Q*.

---

    48. *Generosity*] Clem imagines himself the allegorical figure of magnanimity and good breeding.
    51. *Christen*] Christian.
    54. *feeling*] with pun on the slang word for "bribe" or "tip."
    57. *doom*] judgment.   64. *sweet*] fresh, clear.

BESS.

A censure too severe for Christians.
Great King, I'll pay their ransom.

MULLISHEG.   Thou, my Bess?   70
Thy word shall be their ransom; th' are discharg'd.—
What grave old man is that?

JOFFER.

A Christian preacher, one that would convert
Your Moors and turn them to a new belief.

MULLISHEG.

Then he shall die, as we are King of Fez.   75

BESS.

For these I only spake; for him I kneel,
If I have any grace with mighty Fez.

MULLISHEG.

We can deny thee nothing, beauteous maid.
A kiss shall be his pardon.

BESS.   Thus I pay't.

CLEM [aside].

Must your black face be smooching my mistress's white lips   80
with a Moorian? I would you had kiss'd her a—

ALCADE.

Ha, how is that, sir?

CLEM.

I know what I say, sir; I would he had kiss'd her a—

ALCADE.

A— what?

CLEM.

A thousand times to have done him a pleasure.   85

Enter Spencer *and* Goodlack.

MULLISHEG.

That kiss was worth the ransom of a king.—
What's he of that brave presence?

BESS.

A gentleman of England and my friend.
Do him some grace for my sake.

---

81. *Moorian*] with a play on "murrain"; *with a murrian* = plague on it!
87. *brave presence*] handsome appearance.

MULLISHEG.

> For thy sake what would not I perform?   90
> He shall have grace and honor. —Joffer, go
> And see him gelded to attend on us.
> He shall be our chief eunuch.

BESS.

> Not for ten worlds! Behold, great King, I stand
> Betwixt him and all danger. —Have I found thee?—   95
> Seize what I have, take both my ship and goods,
> Leave naught that's mine unrifled; spare me him.—
> And have I found my Spencer?

CLEM.

> Please your majesty, I see all men are not capable of honor.
> What he refuseth, may it please you to bestow on me.   100

MULLISHEG.

> With all my heart. Go, bear him hence, Alcade,
> Into our Alkedavy. Honor him,
> And let him taste the razor.

CLEM.

> There's honor for me!

ALCADE.

> Come, follow.   105

CLEM

> No, sir; I'll go before you for mine honor.

> > *Exit* [Clem, *with* Alcade].

SPENCER.

> Oh, show yourself, renowned King, the same
> Fame blazons you. Bestow this maid on me;
> 'Tis such a gift as kingdoms cannot buy.
> She is a precedent of all true love   110
> And shall be register'd to after times,
> That ne'er shall pattern her.

GOODLACK.

> Heard you the story of their constant love,
> 'Twould move in you compassion.

ROUGHMAN.

> Let not intemperate love sway you 'bove pity,   115
> That foreign nations that ne'er heard your name

116. nations] *this edn.* (*Dyce's notes*);
nation *Q.*

---

110. *precedent*] model.   112. *pattern*] succeed in copying.

May chronicle your virtues.

MULLISHEG.

You have waken'd in me an heroic spirit;
Lust shall not conquer virtue. —Till this hour
We grac'd thee for thy beauty, Englishwoman,   120
But now we wonder at thy constancy.

BESS.

Oh, were you of our faith, I'd swear great Mullisheg
To be a god on earth. —And lives my Spencer?
In troth I thought thee dead.

SPENCER.   In hope of thee,
I liv'd to gain both life and liberty.   125

Enter Clem *running.*

CLEM.

No more of your honor, if you love me! Is this your Moorish
preferment, to rob a man of his best jewels?

MULLISHEG.

Hast thou seen our Alkedavy?

CLEM.

Davy do you call him? He may be call'd shavy; I am sure
he hath tickled my current commodity. No more your   130
cutting honor, if you love me.

MULLISHEG [*to* Spencer].

All your strange fortunes we will hear discours'd
And after that your fair espousals grace,
If you can find a man of your belief
To do that grateful office.

SPENCER.   None more fit   135
Than this religious and grave gentleman,
Late rescued from death's sentence.

PREACHER.   None more proud
To do you that poor service.

MULLISHEG.   Noble Englishman,

---

130. *current commodity*] popular article, with bawdy allusion and pun on
currant = testicle.

130. *No more your*] Dyce's notes emend to *more o'* and Bates reads *more of,*
but listings in the *OED* (s.v. "No more") suggest that the *of* sometimes
disappeared in colloquial speech.

135. *grateful*] welcome, agreeable.

I cannot fasten bounty to my will
Worthy thy merit. Move some suit to us.   140

SPENCER.

To make you more renown'd, great King, and us
The more indebted, there's an Englishman
Hath forfeited his ship for goods uncustom'd—

MULLISHEG.

Thy suit is granted ere it be half begg'd;
Dispose them at thy pleasure.

SPENCER.   Mighty King,   145
We are your highness' servants.

MULLISHEG.

Come, beauteous maid, we'll see thee crown'd a bride.
At all our pompous banquets these shall wait.
Thy followers and thy servants press with gold,
And not the mean'st that to thy train belongs   150
But shall approve our bounty. Lead in state,
And wheresoe'er thy fame shall be enroll'd,
The world report thou art a girl worth gold.   [*Exeunt.*]

Explicit Actus quintus.

FINIS.

---

140. *Move*] propose.
143. *uncustom'd*] on which no duty has been paid.

THE FAIR MAID OF THE WEST

Part II

To the True Favorer of the Muses and All Good Arts, Thomas Hammon, Esquire, of Gray's Inn, &c.

The first part of this work I bestowed upon your friend
Mr. John Othow; the second I have conferr'd upon you, both
being incorporated into one house and noble society, the   5
proximity in your chambers and much familiar conference
having bred a mutual correspondency betwixt you. The
prime motive inviting me to this dedication, the much love
and many courtesies reflecting upon me from you both,
being the rather encouraged thereunto, that though the sub-   10
ject itself carry no great countenance in the title, yet it hath
not only pass'd the censure of the plebe and gentry, but of the
patricians and *prætextatæ*, as also of our royal Augustus and
Livia. The reason why I have selected you my patrons was to
exclude myself from the number of those of whom Juvenal   15
speaks, Satire 7:

> *Scire volunt omnes, mercedem solvere nemo.*

Please you at any of your more leisur'd hours to vouchsafe
the perusal of these slight papers, your acceptance shall be

0.2. *Thomas Hammon*] Hammon (Hamond) was born about 1592 and
entered Gray's Inn from Christ's College in 1611. He became a barrister in
1617 (J. A. Venn, *Alumni Cantabrigiensis*). In addition to *2 Fair Maid*, Heywood dedicated *1 Iron Age* (1632) to Hammon and directed to him the
epistle which he provided for the 1633 edition of Marlowe's *Jew of Malta*,
saying there that none could claim "more power or privilege" over him
than this friend. Hammon, in his turn, contributed a plate to Heywood's
Hierarchie of the Blessed Angels (1635).

7. *correspondency*] agreement, similarity of mind.

11. *countenance*] credit or repute in the world (*OED*).

12. *plebe*] common people.

13. *prætextatæ*] magistrates. Heywood perhaps means the important people
of the court.

13–14. *Augustus and Livia*] i.e., Charles I and his queen, Henrietta Maria.

17. *Scire . . . nemo*] i.e., *Nosse volunt . . .* ("These are the things which
everyone wants to know, but for which no one is willing to pay"—Ramsay
trans.). Juvenal condemns his age for neglecting men of true learning
(including lawyers and rhetoricians, as Othow and Hammon are); their
knowledge is desired, but no one wants to pay their professional fees. His play,
Heywood says, is the fee he owes to Hammon and Othow for their love and
courtesies; he desires no recompense from them other than their acceptance.

my recompense. Receive my wishes for your earth's happi- 20
ness in millions, for your heaven's bliss in myriads. Taking
my leave of you with that in *Adelph*:

> *Nunquam ita magnifice quicquam dicam,*
> *Id virtus quin superet tua.*

Yours, plenally devoted, 25
THOMAS HEYWOOD

23–24. *Nunquam . . . tua*] "My most splendid phrases must fall short of
your goodness" (Terence, *The Brothers* [*Adelphoe*], II.57. Sargeaunt trans.).
25. *plenally*] fully.

To the Reader

Courteous Reader, if thou beest tired in the first part, I would not wish thee to be travell'd in the second; but I hope much better and that thou didst leave in the last as one that came late to his inn to rest himself for that night only with purpose to go on with the second, as he that riseth early the 5
next morning (having refresh'd himself) to proceed on his journey. By this time you cannot choose but be acquainted with the most of our acts, but not with all, and more particularly for Spencer and his western Bess. With these countrymen of ours in their fellowship, you have heard the beginning 10
of their troubles, but are not yet come to the end of their travels, in which you may accompany them on land without the prejudice of deep ways or robbers and by sea free from the danger of rocks or pirates, as neither using horse or ship more than this book in thine hand and thy chair in thy 15
chamber. More compliment I purpose not, and (I hope) thou expectest not. Farewell.

One studious to be thine,

T. H.

---

2. *travell'd*] (1) caused to make a journey; (2) travailed, wearied. "Travel" and "travail" ordinarily are interchangable, as in 1.12.

3. *leave*] leave off.

13. *prejudice*] injury.

13. *deep ways*] muddy roads.

DRAMATIS PERSONAE

Tota, *Queen of Fez and wife of Mullisheg*, by Theophilus Bourne
Bashaw Joffer
Roughman
Clem, *the clown*
Mullisheg, *King of Fez*   5
Bashaw Alcade, by Mr. Anthony Turner
Mr. Spencer
Captain Goodlack
Forset
Bess Bridges   10
A Porter *of the king's gate*
A Lieutenant *of the Moors*
A Guard [*of Moors*]
A Negro
A Chorus   15
A Captain of the Banditti
The Duke of Florence, *with followers*, by Mr. John Somner
The Duke of Mantua, by Robert Axall
The Duke of Ferrara, by Christopher Goad
A Merchant   20
Two Florentine Lords
Petro Deventuro, *general at sea for the Duke of Florence*
[A Headsman, a Drawer, Moors, Messengers, and Sailors]

20. A Merchant] *this edn.*; *An*   22. Petro Deventuro] *this edn.*;
English Merchant Q.   Pedro Venturo *Q.*

0.1 *Dramatis Personae*] See Appendix B.

3. *Roughman*] spelled *Ruffman* throughout Part II in Q.

9. *Forset*] mute in Part II, although he is alluded to and may enter with
Spencer at III.ii.62.1.

20. *A Merchant*] Although Q specifies an English Merchant, he is, as he
says at IV.i.122, the Italian Merchant of Part I.

21. *Two Florentine Lords*] One Lord is required at V.iii.69.1. He and the
other mentioned here probably make up Florence's train.

The Fair Maid of the West

or

A Girl Worth Gold

PART II

[I.i]   *Enter* Tota, Mullisheg's *Wife*.

TOTA.

    It must not, may not, shall not be endur'd.
    Left we for this our country? To be made
    A mere neglected lady here in Fez,
    A slave to others, but a scorn to all?
    Can womanish ambition, heat of blood,   5
    Or height of birth brook this and not revenge?
    Revenge? On whom? On mighty Mullisheg?
    We are not safe then. On the English stranger?
    And why on her when there's no apprehension
    That can in thought pollute her innocence?   10
    Yet something I must do. What? Nothing yet?
    Nor must we live neglected. I should doubt
    I were a perfect woman, but degenerate
    From mine own sex, if I should suffer this.
    I have a thousand projects in my brain,   15
    But can bring none to purpose.

Enter Bashaw Joffer.

JOFFER.   Call'd your majesty?

TOTA.

    No; yet I think I did. Begone; yet stay.—

---

3. *mere*] completely.
9. *apprehension*] idea.

[*Aside.*]   Will not this misshap'd embryon grow to form?
Not yet? Nor yet?
JOFFER.   I attend your highness' pleasure.
TOTA [*aside*].
    'Tis perfect, and I ha' it.   20
    I am ambitious but to think upon't,
    And if it prove as I have fashion'd it,
    I shall be trophied ever.
JOFFER.   I wait still.
TOTA [*aside*].
    The king no way in peril, she secure,
    None harm'd, all pleas'd, I sweetly satisfied   25
    And yet reveng'd at full. Brain, I for this
    Will wreathe thee in a glorious arch of gold
    Stuck full of Indian gems. But, Tota, whom
    Wilt thou employ in this? The Moors are treacherous,
    And them we dare not trust.
JOFFER.   You need not me.   30
TOTA.
    Say, where's the king?
JOFFER.   I'th' presence.
TOTA.   How?
JOFFER.
    Distempered late and strangely humorous;
    The cause none can conjecture.
TOTA [*aside*].
    Send in his sweetheart,
    And were his own heart double-ribb'd with brass,   35
    Yet she would search the inmost of his thoughts.
    No, 'tis not her on whom I build my project.—
    Is the king upon his entrance?
JOFFER   'Tis thought he is.
    If so, this sudden strange distemperature
    Hath not his purpose altered.
TOTA.   You have now leave   40
    To leave us and attend the king.

---

18. *embryon*] embryo.   23. *trophied*] memorialized.
31. *presence*] presence-chamber.
32. *humorous*] moody, ill-humored.

JOFFER.   I shall.

TOTA.

    If any of the English lady's train
    Come in your way, you may request them hither.
    Say we would question some things of their country.

JOFFER.

    Madam, I shall.   45

TOTA.

    Then on to your attendance. —[*Aside.*]   What we must,
    We'll work by th'English; these we dare not trust.

           Enter Clem *meeting* Joffer.

JOFFER.

    'Tis the queen's pleasure you attend her.

CLEM.

    The queen speak with me? Can you tell the business? A
    murrain of these barbers of Barbary! They have given me a   50
    receipt, that, 'scape the colic as well as I can, I shall be sure
    never to be troubled with the stone.

JOFFER.

    Yonder she walks. I leave ye.   [*Exit.*]

TOTA.

    Now, sir, you are of England?

CLEM.

    And I think you are a witch.   55

TOTA.

    How, sirrah?

CLEM.

    A foolish proverb we use in our country, which, to give you
    in other words, is as much as to say you have hit the nail on
    the head.

TOTA.

    And servant to the English Elizabeth,   60
    So great in court by mighty Mullisheg?
    You follow her?

---

50. *murrain of*] plague on.
51. *that*] so that.
52. *stone*] (1) kidney stone or gallstone; (2) testicle.

CLEM.

> I must confess I am not her gentleman usher to go before her,
> for that way, as the case stands with me now, I can do her
> but small pleasure. I do follow her.   65

TOTA.

> You have seen both nations, England and our Fez.
> How do our people differ?

CLEM.

> Our countrymen eat and drink as yours do for all the
> world; open their eyes when they would see and shut them
> again when thĕy would sleep; when they go, they set one leg   70
> before another; and gape when their mouths open, as yours;
> eat when they have stomachs, scratch when it itcheth. Only
> I hold our nation to be the cleanlier.

TOTA.

> Cleanlier? Wherein?

CLEM.

> Because they never sit down to meat with such foul hands   75
> and faces.

TOTA.

> But how your ladies and choice gentlewomen?

CLEM.

> You shall meet some of them sometimes as fresh as flowers in
> May and as fair as my mistress, and within an hour the same
> gentlewoman as black as yourself or any of your Morians.   80

TOTA.

> Can they change faces so? Not possible.
> Show me some reason for't.

CLEM.

> When they put on their masks.

TOTA.

> Masks? What are they?

71–72. open, as yours; eat] *Collier*;
open, as yours eate *Q*.

---

63. *gentleman usher*] a man of gentle birth who attended one of higher
rank, but Clem alludes to the reputation such courtiers had for becoming
the lovers of the ladies they served. Hence his obscene pun on *go* (1. 63),
which, taken innocently, means "walk."
72. *stomachs*] appetites.

CLEM.

Please you to put off yours and I'll tell you.   85

TOTA.

We wear none but that which nature hath bestowed on us
and our births give us freely.

CLEM.

And our ladies wear none but what the shops yield and they
buy for their money.

TOTA.

Canst thou be secret to me, Englishman?   90

CLEM.

Yes, and chaste too; I have ta'en a medicine for't.

TOTA.

Be fix'd to me in what I shall employ thee,
Constant and private unto my designs,
More grace and honor I will do to thee
Than e'er thou didst receive from Mullisheg.   95

CLEM.

Grace and honor? His grace and honor was to take away
some part, and she would honor me to take away all. I'll see
you damn'd as deep as the black father of your generation,
the devil, first!

TOTA.

Mistake me not.   100

CLEM.

Nay, if you were with child with a young princely devil and
had a mind to any thing that's here, I'd make you lose your
longing.

TOTA.

Sure, this fellow is some sot.

CLEM.

Grace and honor, quotha!   105

Enter Roughman.

ROUGHMAN.

How now, Clem; whither in such post-haste?

---

90. *secret*] (1) private; (2) having to do with the sexual organs. Tota means
(1); Clem puns on (2).

91. *medicine*] potion (i.e., been castrated).

104. *sot*] fool.   105. *quotha*] she says.

CLEM.

> There; if you will have any grace and honor, you may pay
> for't as dear as I have done. 'Sfoot! I have little enough left;
> I would fain carry home something into my own country.

ROUGHMAN.

> Why, what's the matter? I prithee stay.   110

CLEM.

> No, Lieutenant, you shall pardon me, not I; the room is too
> hot for me. I'll be gone; do you stay at your own peril. I'll be
> no longer a prodigal; I'll keep what I have.   *Exit* Clem.

TOTA [*aside*].

> This should have better sense. I'll next prove him.

ROUGHMAN.

> Excuse me, mighty princess, that my boldness   115
> Hath press'd thus far into your privacies.

TOTA.

> You no way have offended. Nay, come near;
> We love to grace a stranger.

ROUGHMAN.   'Twas my ignorance,

> And no pretended boldness.

TOTA.   I have observed you

> To be of some command amongst the English;   120
> Nor make I question but that you may be
> Of fair revenues.

ROUGHMAN.   A poor gentleman.

TOTA.

> We'll make thee rich. Spend that.   [*Gives him money.*]

ROUGHMAN.   Your grace's bounty

> Exceeds what merit can make good in me.
> I am your highness' servant.

TOTA.   Let that jewel   125

> Be worn as our high favor.

ROUGHMAN [*aside*].   'Sfoot! I think

> This queen's in love with me. —Madam, I shall.

TOTA.

> If any favor I can do in court
> Can make you further gracious, speak it freely;
> What power we have is yours.

ROUGHMAN [*aside*].   Doubtless it is so,   130

---

119. *pretended*] intended.

And I am made forever.

TOTA.   Nay, we shall take it ill
To give ourselves so amply to your knowledge,
And you not use us.

ROUGHMAN [*aside*].

Use us! Now upon my life, she's caught.
What, courted by a queen, a royal princess?   135
Where were your eyes, Bess, that you could not see
These hidden parts and mysteries which this queen
Hath in my shape observed? 'Tis but a fortune
That I was born to, and I thank heaven for't.

TOTA.

May I trust you?

ROUGHMAN.   With your life, with your honor.   140
I'll be as private to you as your heart
Within your bosom, close as your own thoughts.—
[*Aside*.] I'll brag of this in England, that I once
Was favorite to a queen. —My royal mistress.

TOTA.

If what you have already promis'd you'll make good,   145
I'll prove so.

ROUGHMAN.   Madam, let this—

TOTA.   What?

ROUGHMAN.   This kiss—

TOTA.

This fool! This ass! This insolent gull!

ROUGHMAN.

Why, did not your grace mean plainly—

TOTA.

In what, sir?

ROUGHMAN.

Did you not court me?   150

TOTA.

How, that face?
Thinkest thou I could love a monkey, a baboon?
Know, were I mounted in the height of lust
And a mere prostitute, rather than thee
I'd embrace one—name but that creature   155
That thou dost think most odious.

ROUGHMAN.   Pardon me, lady;

I humbly take my leave.

TOTA.

Have I given you your description? I pray, sir,
Be secret in't.

ROUGHMAN.   I shall be loth to tell it
Or publish it to any.   160

TOTA.

Yet you are not gone. Know then you have incurr'd
The king's wrath first, our high displeasure next,
The least of which is death. Yet, will you grow
More near to us and prove loyal unto my present purposes,
I will not only pardon you what's past,   165
But multiply my bounties.

ROUGHMAN.   I am your prisoner.

TOTA.

Be free. There's nothing can be call'd offense,
But that in thee we pardon.

ROUGHMAN.   I am fast.

TOTA.

And yet a free man. I am injur'd highly,
And thou must aid me in my just revenge.   170

ROUGHMAN.

Were it to combat the most valiant'st Moor
That ever Fez, Morocco, or Argiers bred,
I for your sake would do it.

TOTA.   We seek nor blood
Nor to expose thee to the least of danger.
I am modest, and what I dare not trust my own tongue with, 175
Or thoughts, I'll boldly give unto thine ears.
List.—   [*Whispers.*]
Do you shake your head? Say, is't done already?

ROUGHMAN.

Wrong my friend?

TOTA.

Do you cast doubts or dangers? Is not our life,   180
Our honor, all in your hand, and will you lavish us,

---

172. *Argiers*] Algiers.
173–174. *nor . . . Nor*] neither . . . nor.   181. *all*] entirely.
181–182. *will . . . excess*] i.e., will you recklessly waste (*lavish*) my life and
honor or reduce (*scant*) my ability to reward you abundantly?

Or scant that bounty should crown you with excess?

ROUGHMAN.

I'll pause upon't.

TOTA.

Is not your life ours by your insolence?
Have not we power to take it?   185

ROUGHMAN.

Say no more; I'll do it.

TOTA.   But may I hope?

ROUGHMAN.

I have cast all doubts and know how it may be compass'd.

TOTA.

There's more gold; your secrecy, that's all I crave.

ROUGHMAN.

To prove myself in this just cause I have,
An honest man or a pernicious knave.   190

TOTA.

Take the advantage of this night.

ROUGHMAN.

I shall expect fair end.
All doubts are cast.

TOTA.   So make a queen thy friend.   *Recorders.*

Enter Mullisheg, Joffer, *and* Alcade, Spencer, Goodlack, Bess, *and the rest.*

MULLISHEG.

All music's harsh; command these discords cease,
For we have war within us.

BESS.   Mighty King,   195
What is't offends your highness?

MULLISHEG.   Nothing, Bess.
Yet all things do. —[*Aside.*]   Oh, what did I bestow
When I gave her away?

BESS.   The queen attends you.

MULLISHEG.

Let her attend.

TOTA [*aside*].   Ay, King, neglected still?
My just revenge shall wound, although not kill.   200

---

187. *compass'd*] devised, executed.

MULLISHEG [*aside*].

    I was a traitor to my own desires

    To part with her so slightly. What, no means

    To alter these proceedings?

SPENCER [*to* Goodlack].   Strange disturbances.

GOODLACK.

    What might the project be?

ALCADE.

    May it please your highness, shall the masque go forward, 205

    That was intended to grace this jovial night?

MULLISHEG.

    We'll have none. Let it be treason held

    To any man that shall but name our pleasure

    Or that vain word delight. —[*Aside.*] The more I gaze,

    The more I surfeit, and the more I strive   210

    To free me from these fires, I am deeper wrapp'd.

    In flames I burn.

SPENCER.

    Your discontent, great prince, takes from us all

    The edge of mirth. These nuptial joys, that should

    Have swell'd our souls with all the sweet varieties   215

    Of apprehensive wishes, with your sadness

    Grows dull and leaden.

    They have lost their taste. In this your discontent

    All pleasures lose their sweetness.

BESS.   Mighty Fez,

    Hath any ignorant neglect in us   220

    Bred these disturbances?

MULLISHEG.   Offense and you

    Are like the warring elements, oppos'd.—

    [*Aside.*] And Fez, why a king and not command thy

       pleasure?

    Is she not within our kingdom? Nay, within our palace

    And therefore in our power? Is she alone   225

    That happiness that I desire on earth?

    Which, since the heavens have given up to mine hands,

---

   204. *project*] notion, idea (i.e., what is he thinking of? *or* what is going on?).

   216. *apprehensive*] quick, discerning.

Shall I despise their bounty and not rather
Run through a thousand dangers to enjoy
Their prodigal favors? Dangers? Tush, there's none.   230
We are here amidst our people, wall'd with subjects round,
And danger is our slave; besides, our war
Is with weak woman. Oh, but I have sworn
And seal'd to her safe conduct. What of that?
Can a king swear against his own desires,   235
Whose welfare is the sinews of his realm?
I should commit high treason 'gainst myself
Not to do that might give my soul content
And satisfy my appetite with fulness. —Alcade.

ALCADE.

    My lord?   240

                                    [*They speak apart.*]

MULLISHEG.

    Rides the English *Negro* still within the harbor?

ALCADE.

    Some league from land.

MULLISHEG.

    Lest that these English should attempt escape
    Now they are laden fully with our bounties,
    Cast thou a watchful eye upon these two.   245

ALCADE.

    I shall.

MULLISHEG.

    I know their love's so fervent and entire,
    They will not part asunder, she leave him
    Or he without her make escape to sea.
    Then while the one's in sight our hopes are safe.   250
    Be that thy charge.

ALCADE.   I'll be an Argus o'er them.

GOODLACK [*aside*].

    Unless the king be still in love with Bess,
    Repenting him of their late marriage,
    'Tis beyond wonder to calculate these storms.

---

251. *Argus*] a giant in Greek mythology who had a hundred eyes; hence,
the emblem of vigilance.

254. *calculate*] reckon up, understand.

MULLISHEG.

How goes the hour?   255

ALCADE.

About some four.

MULLISHEG.

We rose too soon, Bess, from your nuptial feasts.
Something we tasted made us stomach sick,
But now we find a more contentful change.

BESS.

Your sunshine is our day.

MULLISHEG.   Dispose yourselves   260
All to your free desires; to dancing some,
Others to mount our stately Barbary horse,
So famous through the world for swift career,
Stomach, and fiery pace. Those that love arms,
Mount for the tilt.   265
This day is yours; to you 'tis consecrate.
He commits treason in the highest degree
Whose cloudy brow dares the least tempest show
To cross what we intend. Pleasure shall spring
From us to flow on you.

ALL.   Long live the king!   270

MULLISHEG.

To your free pastimes; leave us. —Captain, stay.

Exeunt. Manet Goodlack [*with* Mullisheg].

Captain, I read a fortune in thy brow
More than the slight presage of augury,
Which tells me thou, and only thou, art mark'd
To make me earthly bless'd.

GOODLACK.   That I can do't?   275

MULLISHEG.

It lies in thee to raise thy ruin'd fortunes
As high as is a viceroy's, wreathe thy front

---

263. *career*] "the short turning of a nimble horse, now this way, nowe that
way" (1573; *OED*).

264. *Stomach*] high spirit.

271.1. *Manet Goodlack*] Goodlack remains.   272. *brow*] countenance.

273. *presage of augury*] indication from tokens predicting the future (i.e.,
he has noticed a general inclination on Goodlack's part to advance himself;
now he pretends to see something specific).

277. *front*] forehead.

−108−

Within a circled piramis of gold,
And to command in all our territories
Next to our person.

GOODLACK.   Golden promises.   280

MULLISHEG.

Our words are acts, our promises are deeds;
We do not feed with air. It lies in thee;
We two may grapple souls, be friends and brothers.

GOODLACK.

Teach me how.

MULLISHEG.

I do not find thee coming; in thy looks   285
I cannot spy that fresh alacrity,
Which with a glad and sprightful forwardness
Should meet our love half way.

GOODLACK.   You wonder me.

MULLISHEG.

No, thou art dull or fearful. Fare thee well.
Thou hadst a fate laid up to make thee chronicled   290
In thy own country, but thou wilt basely lose it
Even by thine own neglect.

GOODLACK.   Forspeak me not.
The sun ne'er met the summer with more joy
Than I'd embrace my fortunes, but to you,
Great King, to whom I am so greatly bound,   295
I'd purchas't with a danger should fright earth,
Astonish heaven, and make all hell to tremble.
I am of no shrinking temper.

MULLISHEG.

Prove but as wise as thou art bold and valiant
And gain me wholly to thee. Half thou hast already   300
Purchas'd by this bold answer; but perform
The rest, and we are all and only thine.

GOODLACK.

Show me the way to gain this royal purchase.
If I do't not, divide me from your presence,
From your grace, and all those glorious hopes   305

---

278. *piramis*] pyramid (i.e., crown).
285. *coming*] ready, eager.   292. *Forspeak*] renounce.
294–296. *to you . . . purchas't*] bring it about for you. . . .

You have propos'd turn into scorns and scandals.

MULLISHEG.

    I am dull and drowsy on the sudden.
    Whilst I sleep, Captain, read there.

                 He counterfeits sleep and gives him a letter.

GOODLACK [*reads*].

    "To make Bess mine, some secret means devise.
    To thy own height and heart I'll make thee rise."   310
    Is not this ink the blood of basilisks
    That kills me in the eyes and blinds me so
    That I can read no further? 'Twas compos'd
    Of dragons' poison and the gall of asps,
    Of serpents' venom or of vipers' stings;   315
    It could not read so harsh else. Oh, my fate!
    Nothing but this? This? Had a parliament
    Of fiends and furies in a synod sat
    And devis'd, plotted, parlied, and contriv'd,
    They scarce could second this. This? 'Tis unparallel'd.   320
    To strumpet a chaste lady, injure him
    That rates her honor dearer than his life;
    T'employ a friend in treasons 'gainst his friend
    And put that friend to do't; t'impose on me
    The hateful style and blot of pandarism   325
    That am a gentleman; nay, worse than this,
    Make me in this a traitor to my country
    In giving up their honors. Who but a Moor,
    Of all that bears man's shape likest a devil,
    Could have devis'd this horror? Possible   330
    That he should mark out me? What does my face
    Prognosticate that he should find writ there
    An index of such treasons? But beware.
    'Twas his own plot, ay, and his cunning too;
    I'll add that to his project. But a viceroy   335
    And a king's minion, titles that will shadow
    Ills the most base and branded. Not to do it
    May purchase his displeasure, which can be

---

311. *basilisks*] fabulous serpents whose looks could kill.
333. *index*] the table of contents of a book (i.e., an indicator).
336. *minion*] favorite.

No less than death or bondage. Here's propos'd
Honor and peril. But what writes he further?   340
"We are impatient of delays; this night
Let it be done." I am doubtful of my purpose
And can resolve of nothing.

                    Mullisheg *starts out of his chair as from a dream.*

MULLISHEG.   If he fail
I'll have his flesh cut small as winter's snow
Or summer's atoms.

GOODLACK.   Ha, was that by us?   345

MULLISHEG.

Where was I? —Oh, I dream'd upon the sudden.
How fast was I!

GOODLACK [*aside*].   A fair warning 'twas.
Have you the cunning to speak your thoughts in dreams?

MULLISHEG.

Who's i'th' next room?

GOODLACK.

My lord.   350

MULLISHEG.

My Captain, was it thou?
Sleep did surprise my senses, worthy friend,
And in my dreams I did remember thee.

GOODLACK.

How, me, my lord?

MULLISHEG.

Methought I had employ'd thee in a business   355
In which thou wert or fearful or else false,
At which I was so overcome with rage
That from my dreams I started.

GOODLACK [*aside*].   Seamen say,
When halcyons sing, look for a storm that day.

---

345. *atoms*] motes of dust.   345. *by us*] i.e., intended for me.
356. *or . . . or*] either . . . or.
359. *halcyons*] sea birds "said to build their nests and hatch their young on
the heaving billows, and to utter shrill cries of warning to the seamen when-
ever a storm threatened . . ." (H. A. Guerber, *Myths of Greece and Rome*
[1893], p. 212).

There's death in my denial.

MULLISHEG.   Did you read   360
   That scroll we gave you, Captain? There's wrapp'd up
   A thousand honors for thee and more gold
   Than, shouldst thou live a double Nestor's age,
   Thou couldst find ways to lavish.

GOODLACK.

   Add to your work a business of more danger   365
   That I may think me worthy; otherwise,
   This slight employment will but prize me low
   And of desertless merit.

MULLISHEG.   Think'st thou, Captain,
   It may be easily compass'd?

GOODLACK.   Dare you trust me?

MULLISHEG.

   I dare.

GOODLACK.   Then know, besides to dare and can,   370
   I will, though work beyond the power of man.
   I'll set my brains in action.

MULLISHEG.   Noble friend,
   Above thy thoughts our honors shall extend.

GOODLACK.

   I am not to be shaken.

MULLISHEG.   Where be our eunuchs?
   We'll crown our hopes and wishes with more pomp   375
   And sumptuous cost than Priam did his son's
   That night he bosom'd Helen; she's as fair,
   And we'll command our pomp to be as rare.
   We will have torches shall exceed the stars
   In number and in brightness. We will have   380
   Rare change of music shrill and high
   That shall exceed the spheres in harmony.

---

363. *Nestor's age*] Nestor was a warrior who fought with the Greeks
against the Trojans. The *Iliad* makes him about seventy, but he was often
depicted (as in Shakespeare's *Troilus*) as being indefinitely antique.

376–377. *Priam . . . Helen*] According to some versions of the story, King
Priam of Troy celebrated the nuptials of his son Paris and the Greek Helen
with "feste and gret solempnyte . . . Through-oute the toun be viii dayes
space" (Lydgate's *Troy Book*, ed. Bergen, II, 4175 ff.).

382. *spheres*] the globes encircling the earth and incorporating the
heavenly bodies, which in their revolutions emitted notes that combined
into a celestial music.

The jewels of her habit shall reflect
To daze all eyes that shall behold her state.
Our treasure shall, like to a torrent, rush   385
Streams of rewards richer than Tagus' sands
To make these English strangers swim in gold.
In wild moriscos we will lead the bride,
And when with full satieties of pleasures
We are dull and satiate, at her radiant eyes   390
Kindle fresh appetite, since they aspire
T'exceed in brightness the high orbs of fire.
Make this night mine, as we are King of Fez,
Th'art viceroy, Captain.   *Exit* Mullisheg.

GOODLACK.   Make my estate much less
And my attempts more honorable. Honor and virtue   395
To me seem things in opposition,
Nor can we with small danger catch at one,
But we must lose the other. Oh my brain,
In what a labyrinth art thou! Say I could
Be false, as he would make me, what device,   400
What plot, what train have I to compass it?
Or with what face can I solicit her
In treason towards my friend?

Enter Roughman.

ROUGHMAN [*aside*].
I am to solicit Spencer
To lie with the Moor's queen, a business Bess   405
Will hardly thank me for; but howsoever
I have underta'en it.
GOODLACK [*aside*].
Impossibilities all. The more I wade,
The more I drown in weakness.
ROUGHMAN.
Captain.   410
GOODLACK.
Oh, Lieutenant,

---

386. *Tagus*'] The Tagus is a Spanish river, supposed to be rich in gold.
388. *moriscos*] morris-dances, supposed to have originated with the Moors
because some dancers wore blackface.
392. *orbs of fire*] heavenly bodies.   401. *train*] scheme.

Never was man perplex'd thus.

ROUGHMAN.   What, as you?

    Had you but my disturbance in your brain,

    'Twould tax a stoic's wit or Œdipus'.

    Why, Captain, a whole school of sophisters   415

    Could not unriddle me.

GOODLACK.

    I would we might change business.

ROUGHMAN.

    I would give boot so to be rid of mine.

GOODLACK.

    Shall we be free and open breasted?

ROUGHMAN.   How?

GOODLACK.

    As thus: 420

    Tell me thy grievances, and unto thee

    I will unveil my bosom. Both disclos'd,

    I'll beg in mine thy counsel and assistance;

    Thy cause shall mine command.

ROUGHMAN.   A heart, a hand.

GOODLACK.

    I am to woo fair Bess to lie with Mullisheg.   425

ROUGHMAN.

    And I woo Spencer to embrace the queen.

GOODLACK.

    Is't possible?

ROUGHMAN.

    'Tis more than possible; 'tis absolutely pass'd.

GOODLACK.

    There's not a hair to choose. Canst counsel me?

414–415. *stoic's . . . sophisters*] *Stoics* were adherents of a philosophical school founded by Zeno (the allusion here is to the intricacy of their philosophical argument). *Œdipus* answered a famous riddle put to him by the Sphinx. A *sophister* was a sophist, a professional teacher of philosophy in ancient Greece or, more generally, a learned man; in Renaissance England the term was applied (as here, perhaps) to a second- or third-year student at Cambridge.

418. *boot*] something into the bargain.   428. *pass'd*] decreed.

ROUGHMAN.

Can you advise me?

GOODLACK.   I am past my wits.   430

ROUGHMAN.

And I beyond all sense.

GOODLACK.

Wouldst thou do't, here lay the way plain before thee?

ROUGHMAN.

What, for gold betray my friend and country?
Would you, Captain?

GOODLACK.   What, and wear a sword
To guard my honor and a Christian's faith?   435
I'd flesh it here first.

ROUGHMAN.   Nobly resolved.

GOODLACK.

We are not safe, Lieutenant. Moors are treacherous. *they were praising them before*
Nay, come, thy counsel. Fez hath proffer'd me
The honor of a viceroy, and withal,
If I should fail performance, cunningly   440
Hath threaten'd me with death.

ROUGHMAN.   You still propose
The danger, but you show no way to clear them.

GOODLACK.

Brain, let me waken thee. 'Sfoot, hast thou
No project? Dost thou partake my dulness?

ROUGHMAN.

The more I strive, the more I am entangled.   445

GOODLACK.

And I, too. Not yet?

ROUGHMAN.   Nor yet, nor ever.

GOODLACK.

'Twas coming here, and now again 'tis vanish'd.

ROUGHMAN.

Call't back again, for heaven's sake.

GOODLACK.   Again.

ROUGHMAN.

Thanks, heaven!

GOODLACK.   And now again 'tis gone.

ROUGHMAN.

    Can you not catch fast hold on't?

GOODLACK.   Give me way;   450

    Let's walk, Lieutenant. Could a man propose

    A stratagem to gull this lustful Moor,

    To supply him and then to satiate her?

ROUGHMAN.

    Good.

GOODLACK.

    Next, out of all these dangers secure us   455

    And keep our treasure safe.

ROUGHMAN.   'Twere excellent.

GOODLACK.

    But how shall this be done?

ROUGHMAN.

    Why, Captain, know not you?

GOODLACK.

    Think'st thou it in the power of man to work it?

    Yet come, I'll try; I owe my fate a death.   460

    Be sway'd by me in all things.

ROUGHMAN.   Noble Captain,

    I do not wish to outlive thee.   [*Exeunt.*]

             Explicit Actus primus.

[II.i]   *Enter* Spencer, Bess, *and* Clem.

SPENCER.

    The king was wondrous pleasant. Oh my Bess,

    How much am I indebted to his highness

    Only for gracing thee.

BESS.   Could my Spencer

    Think that a barbarous Moor could be so train'd

    In human virtues?   5

CLEM.

    Fie upon't! I am so tir'd with dancing with these same black

    she chimney sweepers that I can scarce set the best leg for-

    ward; they have so tir'd me with their moriscos, and I have

---

450. *Give me way*] give me room; do not press me for an answer.

so tickled them with our country dances, Sellenger's round
and Tom Tiler. We have so fiddled it!   10

SPENCER.

Sirrah, what news will you tell to your friends when you
return into England?

CLEM.

Brave news, which, though I can neither write nor read, yet
I have committed them to my tables and the rest of my
memory.   15

SPENCER.

Let's hear some of your novelties.

CLEM.

First and foremost, I have observed the wisdom of these
Moors, for some two days since, being invited to one of the
chief bashaws to dinner, after meat sitting by a huge fire and
feeling his shins to burn, I requested him to pull back his   20
chair, but he very understandingly sent for three or four
masons and removed the chimney. The same Morian
entreated me to lie with him, and I, according to the state of
my travels, willing to have a candle burning by, but he by no
means would grant it. I ask'd him why. "No," says he,   25
"we'll put out the light that the fleas may not know where
to find us."

Enter Goodlack *and* Roughman.

SPENCER.

No storm at sea could be so tyrannous
Nor half th'affright bear in his forehead bare
As I spy in that look.   30

BESS.

Let not your looks presage more terrors than
Your tongues can speak. Out with't at once, Lieutenant.

9–10. *Sellenger's round . . . Tom Tiler*] popular fiddler's tunes.

14–15. *tables . . . memory*] Clem is quibbling on tables = a notebook for
memoranda, and tables = *tabulae*, alluding to Aristotle's assertion that the
pristine state of the mind is that of a *tabula rasa*, a blank tablet.

21. *understandingly*] intelligently.

23–24. *according . . . travels*] The state of Clem's travels (the special treatment accorded him as a guest) would entitle him to the luxury of a candle;
the state of his travails (the apprehension arising from sleeping in a strange
place) would make a candle desirable.

SPENCER.   Captain, speak.

GOODLACK.   W'are all lost.

ROUGHMAN.   All shipwreck'd.

CLEM.

    Are we ashore, and shall we be cast away?

SPENCER.

    Great Mullisheg is royal.

GOODLACK.   False to you.   35

BESS.

    Gracious and kind.

ROUGHMAN.   Disloyal to us all.

SPENCER.

    Wrap me not in these wonders, worthy friend.

    The very doubt of what the danger is,

    Is more than danger can be.

BESS.   Be it death,

    So we may die together. Here's a heart   40

    Fear never could affright.

GOODLACK.

    The king still loves your Bess.

SPENCER.

    Ha?

ROUGHMAN.

    The queen your Spencer.

BESS.

    How?   45

GOODLACK.

    This night he must enjoy her.

ROUGHMAN.   And she him.

SPENCER.

    A thousand deaths are in that word contriv'd.

    I'll make my passage through the blood of kings,

    Rather than suffer this.

BESS.   I through hell,

    Or were there place more dangerous—

GOODLACK.   Else all die.   50

CLEM.

    Die? 'Sfoot, this is worse than being made an eunuch as I

    was.

SPENCER.

We have yet life, and therefore cherish hope.

GOODLACK.

All hopes are banish'd in the deep abyss
Of our perplexed thoughts.

ROUGHMAN.   All things run retrograde.   55

BESS.

Why, Captain, why, Lieutenant, had you the skill
To bring my ship thus far to wreck her here?
Pass'd you the ocean to perish in the harbor?
Thou, Tom Goodlack,
Wert ever true and just to my designs,   60
And canst thou fail me now?

GOODLACK.   I study for you.

BESS.

Hast thou brought me but to see my Spencer's shadow
And not enjoy the substance, for what more
Have I yet had from him than from his picture
That once hung in my chamber? Gentlemen, amongst you all 65
Rescue an innocent maid from violence,
Or do but say it cannot be prevented.
I begin; he that best loves me, follow.

SPENCER.

What means Bess?

GOODLACK [aside].

If it could be fashion'd to my thoughts   70
And have success, 'twere brave.

SPENCER.   What, noble friend?

GOODLACK.

To thrive but as we purpose.

SPENCER.   Have you way?

GOODLACK [aside].

'Tis but a desperate course, and if it fail,
The worst can be but death; and I, even I,
That laid the plot will teach them how to die.   75
I'll lead them on.

SPENCER.   If thou hast any project—

---

74. *but*] nothing except.

BESS.

    Joy or comfort—

ROUGHMAN.   And if not comfort, counsel—

GOODLACK [aside].

    Say it thrive?

SPENCER.

    What, Captain, what?

GOODLACK.   You'll rip it from the womb

    Ere it be fully hatch'd now. —[Aside.] If it prosper   80

    But to my desire and wishes, 'twere admirable.

SPENCER.

    No longer hold us in suspense, good Captain,

    But free us from these fears.

GOODLACK.   You, noble friend,

    This night cast gracious eyes upon the queen.

BESS.

    And prove to me disloyal?

GOODLACK.   Still you cross me   85

    And make the birth abortive. You, fair Bess,

    With amorous favors entertain the king.

SPENCER.

    And yield herself to his intemperate lust?

GOODLACK.

    You still prevent me; either give me way

    To show you light unto your liberties,   90

    Or still remain in darkness.

ROUGHMAN.   Hear him out.

GOODLACK [to Roughman].

    You soothe the queen; I'll flatter with the king.

    Let's promise fair on both sides, say 'tis done

    All to their own desires.

SPENCER.   The event of this?

GOODLACK.

    A happy freedom with a safe escape   95

    Unto our ship this night.

BESS.   Oh, could this be!

GOODLACK.

    Fortune assists the valiant and the bold;

---

89. *prevent*] forestall.

We'll bid fair for't. —I had forgot myself.
Where's Clem?

CLEM.

Noble Captain.   100

GOODLACK.

Post to the ship. Bid Forset man the long boat
With ten good musketeers, and at a watchword,
If we can free our passage, take us in.
Nay, make haste; one minute's stay is death.

CLEM.

I am gone in a twinkling.   [*Exit.*] 105

GOODLACK [*aside*].

To compass the king's signet; then to command
Our passage, 'scape the gates and watches too:
For that I have brain. The king's upon
His entrance. Hours waste; revels come on.
A thousand projects of death, hopes, and fears,   110
Are warring in my bosom, and at once.—
Eye you the queen, and humor you the king;
Let no distaste nor discontented brow
Appear in you. Their lust I'll make the ground
To set all free or keep your honor sound.   115
Disperse; the king's on coming.   *Flourish.*

Enter Mullisheg, Tota, Joffer, *and* Alcade.

MULLISHEG

We consecrate this evening, beauteous bride,
To th' honor of your nuptials.—

[Mullisheg *speaks apart to* Goodlack, Tota *to* Roughman.]

Is all done?

GOODLACK.

Done.

TOTA.   Is he ours?

ROUGHMAN.   Yours.

TOTA.   And we ever thine.

GOODLACK.

Ay, and so cast that she shall grasp you freely   120

---

106. *compass*] obtain deviously.

And thinks she hugs her Spencer.

ROUGHMAN.

And when he bosoms you thinks he enfolds
His lovely Bess.

TOTA.   Thou mak'st a queen thy servant.

GOODLACK.

Your highness' signet to command our passage
From chamber to chamber.

MULLISHEG.   'Tis there.

GOODLACK.   The word.   125

MULLISHEG.

'Tis *Mullisheg*.

GOODLACK [*aside*].

This must bring us safe aboard.

MULLISHEG.   We keep the bride
Too long from rest now; she is free for bed.

TOTA.

Please her to accept it
In honor of her beauty, this night I'll   130
Do her any service.

BESS.   Mighty princess,
Excuse my breeding from such arrogance
And overbold presumption; you nor yours
Can owe me any duty. 'Tis besides
The fashion of our country not to trust   135
The secrets of a nuptial night like this
To the eyes of any stranger.

TOTA.   At your pleasure.

BESS.

With our first night's unlacing, mighty Queen,
We dare not trust our husbands; 'tis a modesty
Our English maids profess.   140

MULLISHEG.

Keep your own customs as you shall think best.
So for this night we leave you to your rest.

TOTA [*to* Roughman].

Remember.

ROUGHMAN.   'Tis writ here.

MULLISHEG [*to* Goodlack].   Captain.

Exeunt. Manet Goodlack.

GOODLACK.   I am fast.

   Now is my task in labor and is plung'd

   In thousand throes of childbirth. Dangerous it is   145

   To deal where kings' affairs are question'd

   Or may be parled; but what's he so base

   That would not all his utmost powers extend

   For freedom of his country and his friend?

   When all the court is silent, sunk in dreams,   150

   Then must my spirits awake. By this the king

   Has ta'en his leave of bride and bridegroom too;

   And th'amorous queen longs for some happy news

   From Roughman, as great Fez expects from us;

   My friend and Bess wrapp'd in a thousand fears   155

   To find my plot in action; and it now

   Must take new life. Auspicious fate, thy aid

   To guard the honor of this English maid.   *Exit.*

[II.ii]   *Enter* Roughman *ushering the* Queen [Tota].

ROUGHMAN.

   Tread soft, good madam.

TOTA.   Is this the chamber?

ROUGHMAN.

   I'll bring him instantly.

   He thinks this bed provided for his Bess

   And that she lodges here, while she, poor soul,

   Embraceth naught but air.   5

TOTA.

   Thou mak'st a queen thy servant.

ROUGHMAN.   Beware;

   Be not too loud, lest that your tongue betrays you.

TOTA.

   Mute as night, as silent and as secret.

   Wrongs should be paid with wrongs, for so indeed 'tis meet;

   My just revenge, though secret, yet 'tis sweet.   10

   Haste time, and hast our bounty.

ROUGHMAN.   Queen, I shall.   [*Exit* Tota.]

152. Has] *Collier*; H'as *Q*.

---

  147. *parled*] debated.

So now were we all safe and in our *Negro* shipp'd,
Might'st thou lie there till doomsday, lustful Queen.   *Exit.*

[II.iii]   *Enter* Goodlack *and the* King [Mullisheg].

GOODLACK.

My lord, the custom is in England still
For maids to go to bed before their husbands;
It saves their cheek from many a modest blush.

KING.

And in the dark?

GOODLACK.   We use it for the most part.

KING.

Soft may their bones lie in their beds of ashes   5
That brought this custom into England first.

GOODLACK.

This the place where Bess expects her Spencer.

KING.

Thou Viceroy of Argiers—for, Captain, that
Is now thy title—thou hast won a king
To be thy breast companion.

GOODLACK.   Not too loud.   10

Why enters not your highness? You are safe.

KING.

With as much joy as to our prophet's rest.
But what thinks Spencer of this?

GOODLACK.

I have shifted in her place a certain Moor
Whom I have hir'd for money, which, poor soul,   15
He entertains for Bess.

KING.   My excellent friend.

GOODLACK.

Beware of conference, lest your tongue reveals
What this safe darkness hides.

KING.   I am all silent.—

---

12. *So*] provided that.
[II.iii]
    12. *prophet's rest*] the delights of the Mohammedan paradise.

> Oh, thou contentful night, into thy arms,
> Of all that e'er I tasted, sweetest and best,   20
> I throw me more for pleasure than for rest.   *Exit* King.

GOODLACK.

> One fury clasp another and there beget
> Young devils between you, so fair Bess be safe.
> I have here the king's signet; this will yield us
> Way through the court and city. Bess being mask'd,   25
> How can she be descried when none suspect,
> Our flight this day not dreamt on? Now to execute
> What was before purpos'd, which if it speed,
> I'll say the heavens have in our fates agreed.   *Exit.*

[II.iv]   *Enter* Bess, Spencer, *and* Roughman.

SPENCER.

> How goes the night?

ROUGHMAN.   'Tis some two hours from day.

BESS.

> Yet no news from the captain.

ROUGHMAN.   I have done
> A midwife's part. I have brought the queen to bed;
> I could do no more.

Enter Goodlack.

SPENCER.   The captain is come.

BESS.   Thy news?

GOODLACK.

> All safe. Faith, wench, I have put them to it for   5
> A single combat; I have left them at it.

BESS.

> King and queen?

GOODLACK.   The same.

ROUGHMAN.   Now for us.

GOODLACK.

> Ay, there's all the danger; there's one bashaw
> Whose eyes is fix'd on Spencer, and he now
> Walks e'en before our lodging.

BESS.   Then what's past   10
> Is all yet to no purpose.

GOODLACK.   He and I
    May freely pass the court, and you, fair Bess,
    I would disguise. But then for Spencer?

BESS.
    Why, that's the main of all; all, without his freedom,
    That we can aim at's nothing.   15

SPENCER.
    It shall be thus, which alter none that loves me.
    With this signet you three shall pass to th' ship;
    Whilst I'm in sight, she will not be suspected.
    My escape leave to my own fair fortunes.

BESS.
    How that?   20

SPENCER.
    Through twenty bashaws I will hew my way,
    But I will see thee ere morning.

BESS.   Think'st thou, Spencer,
    That I will leave thee? Think'st thou that I can?
    Thou mayst as well part body from the soul
    As part us now. It is our wedding night;   25
    Wouldst now divide us?

SPENCER.   Yield to time's necessities,
    And to our strict disasters.

GOODLACK.   Words are vain;
    We now must cleave to action. Our stay's death,
    And if we be not quick in expedition,
    We all perish.   30

SPENCER.
    Bess, be sway'd.

BESS.   To go to sea without thee
    And leave thee subject unto a tyrant's cruelty?
    I'll die a thousand deaths first.

SPENCER.   First save one
    And by degrees the rest. When thou hast pass'd
    The perils of this night, I am half safe,   35
    But whilst thou art still environ'd more than better

---

27. *strict*] severe.
27. *disasters*] misfortunes.
36. *environ'd*] surrounded by enemies.

Half of my part's endanger'd.

GOODLACK.   Talk yourselves
To your deaths, do; will you venter forth?
Leave me to the bashaw.

ROUGHMAN.

Or me; I'll buffet with him for my passage.   40

SPENCER.

Neither; in what I purpose I am constant.
Conduct her safe. Th'advantage of the night
I'll take for my escape, and my sweet Bess,
If in the morning I behold thee not
Safe within my *Negro*, be assur'd   45
I am dead. Nay, now, delays are vain.

BESS.

Sir, did you love me,
You would not stay behind me.

SPENCER.   I'll ha't so.—
Gentlemen, be chary of this jewel
That throws herself into the arms of night   50
Under your conduct. —If I live, my Bess,
Tomorrow I'll not fail thee.

BESS.

And if thou diest tomorrow, be assur'd
Tomorrow I'll be with thee.

SPENCER.   Shall thy love
Betray us all to death?

BESS.   Well, I will go,   55
But if thou dost miscarry, think the ocean
To be my bride bed.

SPENCER.   Heaven for us!
That power that hath preserv'd us hitherto
Will not let's sink now. —And, brave gentlemen,
Of the Moor's bounty bear not any thing   60
Unto our ship, lest they report of us
We fled by night and robb'd them.

GOODLACK.   Nobly resolv'd.

---

37. *part's*] share in the adventure is, function is.

38. *venter*] venture.

39. *Leave . . . bashaw*] Leave the bashaw to me.

SPENCER.

    Now embrace and part, and my sweet Bess,
    This be thy comfort 'gainst all future fears:
    To meet in mirth that now divide in tears.   65
    Farewell, Bess. I'll back into my chamber.   [*Exit.*]

BESS.

    Can I part with life in more distracted horror?

GOODLACK.

    You spoil all that we before have plotted.
    Will you mask yourself? And to the porter first—
    Ho, porter!   70

                Enter Porter.

PORTER.

    Who calls?

GOODLACK.   One from the king.

PORTER.   How shall I know that?

GOODLACK.

    This token be your warrant; behold his signet.

PORTER.

    That's not enough. The word?

GOODLACK.   *Mullisheg.*

PORTER.   Pass freely.

        [*Exeunt* Goodlack, Bess, *and* Roughman.]

    Some weighty business is in hand that the king's signet is
    abroad so late. But no matter; this is my discharge. I'll to my   75
    rest.   *Exit* Porter.

[II.v]   *Enter* Alcade.

ALCADE.

    I much suspect; these English 'mongst themselves are treach-
    erous. I have observ'd the king had conference with the cap-
    tain. Many whisperings and passages I have observed, but
    that which makes me most suspect is because the king hath
    removed his lodging, and it may be to prostitute the English   5
    maid. Ha, suspect, said I? Nay, examine things exactly and't
    must needs be so; the king is woundrous bountiful, and what
    is't gold cannot? Troth, I could even pity the poor forlorn

73. S.P. PORTER.] *Collier*; *not in* Q,   *Goodlack's preceding speech.*
which prints That's . . . word *as part of*

Englishman, who this night must be forc'd t' lie alone and
have the king taste to him.   10

Enter Spencer.

SPENCER [*aside*].

Sure, this Moor hath been made private to the king's intents,
which if I find, I'll make him the instrument for me to pass
the court gates. This man, whose office was to keep me, shall
be the only means to free me.

ALCADE [*aside*].

On his marriage night and up at this hour? Nay, if I once   15
suspect, 'tis as firm as if it were confirmed by Alcoran, or
Mahomet himself had sworn it. I'll sport myself with his
distaste and sorrow.

SPENCER.

Thus abus'd!

ALCADE.

What, up so late and on your bridal night,   20
When you should lie lull'd in the fast embrace
Of your fair mistress? —[*Aside*.]   I hope I have given't him
soundly.

SPENCER.

S'possible
To lodge my bride in one place and dispose me
To a wrong chamber? She not once send to me,   25
That I might know to find her?

ALCADE [*aside*].   Excellent!

Nay, if I once suspect, it never fails.

SPENCER.

I'll not take't
At th' hands of an empress, much less at hers.

ALCADE.

Why, what's the business, sir? Oh, I guess the cause of your   30
grief.

9. forc'd t' lie] *Collier* (forced to lie);
forc't lie *Q*.

---

10. *taste to*] act as a taster (of food, ordinarily) to, with *taste* carrying
overtones of "having carnal knowledge of."
16. *Alcoran*] the Koran, sometimes spoken of, as here, as though it were a
pagan deity.

SPENCER.

And, sir, you may, but I'll be reveng'd.

ALCADE.

Troth, and I would.

SPENCER.   I'll bosom somebody,

Be it the common'st courtesan in Fez,

If not for love, to vex her.

ALCADE.   Can you do less?   35

SPENCER.

To leave me the first night!

ALCADE.   Oh, 'twas a sign

She never dearly lov'd you.

SPENCER.   I perceive,

Bashaw Alcade, you understand my wrongs.

ALCADE.

In part, though not in whole.

SPENCER.

Your word is warrant; pass me the court gate. I'll to some   40

loose bordello and tell her when I have done.

ALCADE.

Were it my cause, I'd do this and more.

SPENCER.

Make me wait thus!

ALCADE.   Oh sir, 'tis insufferable.

SPENCER.

Troth, I dally my revenge too long. —What ho, porter!

[*Enter* Porter.]

PORTER.

How now, who calls?   45

ALCADE.

Here's Bashaw Alcade; turn the key.

PORTER.

His name commands my gate; pass freely.

SPENCER.

Sir, I am bound to you.

To take this wrong, I should be held no man.—

[*Aside.*]   Now to the watch; 'scape there as I can.   *Exit.*   50

ALCADE.

Ha, ha! So long as she sleeps in the arms of Fez, let him

pack where he pleases. —Porter, now he's without, let
him command his entrance no more, neither for reward
nor entreaty, till day breaks.

PORTER.

Sir, he shall not.   55

ALCADE.

'Tis well we are so rid of him.
Mullisheg will give me great thanks for this.
I'll to his chamber, there attend without,
Till he shall waken from his drowsy rest,
And then acquaint him with this fortunate jest.   [*Exit.*]   60

[II.vi]

Alarum. Enter Joffer, *Lieutenant* [*and Watch*], Spencer *prisoner and
wounded.*

JOFFER.

Sir, though we wonder at your noble deeds,
Yet I must do the office of a subject
And take you prisoner. By that noble blood
That runs in these my veins, when I behold
The slaughter you have made, which wonders me,   5
I wish you had escap'd and not been made captive
To him, who though he may admire and love you,
Yet cannot help you.

SPENCER.

Your style is like your birth, for you are Joffer,
Chief bashaw to the king, and him I know   10
Lord of most noble thoughts. Speak; what's my danger?

JOFFER.

Know, sir, a double forfeit of your life.
Your outrage first is death, being in the night
And 'gainst the watch, but those that you have slain
In this fierce conflict brings 'em without all bounds   15
Of pardon.

SPENCER.

I was born to't, and I embrace my fortune.

---

52. *pack*] depart, roam.
[II.vi]
  15. *'em*] i.e., Spencer's two faults.

JOFFER.

Sir, now I know you
To be that brave and worthy Englishman
So highly grac'd in court, which more amazeth me   20
That you should thus requite him with the slaughter
Of his lov'd subjects.

SPENCER.   I entreat you, sir,
As you are noble, question me no further.
I have many private thoughts that trouble me,
And not the fear of death.

JOFFER.   We know your name   25
And now have prov'd your courage: both these moves us
To give you as easy bondage as our loyalty
To the king can suffer. You are free from irons.

SPENCER [aside].

When this news shall come to her—

OFFER.

Lieutenant, lead the watch some distance off;   30
Bid them remove these bodies lately slain.
I must have private conference with this prisoner.
Leave him to my charge.—   [Exeunt Lieutenant and Watch.]
                         Sir, think me, though a Moor,
A nation strange unto you Christians,
Yet that I can be noble; but in you   35
I have observ'd strange contrarieties,
Which I would be resolv'd in.

SPENCER.   Speak your thoughts.

JOFFER.

When I conferr'd the nobleness of your blood
With this your present passion, I much muse
Why either such a small effuse of blood,   40
These your slight wounds, or the pale fear of death
Should have the power to force a tear from such
A noble eye.

SPENCER.

Why, think'st thou, Bashaw, that wounds, blood, or death
Could force a tear from me? Thou noblest of thy nation,   45

---

21. *him*] i.e., Mullisheg.
38. *conferr'd*] compared.

Do not so far misprize me. I tell thee, Bashaw,
The rack, strappado, or the scalding oil,
The burning pincers, or the boiling lead,
The stakes, the pikes, the cauldron, or the wheel,
Were all these tortures to be felt at once,   50
Could not draw water hence.

JOFFER.   Whence comes it then?

SPENCER.

From that whose pains as far surmounts all those
As whips of Furies do the ladies' fans
Made of the plumes o'th' estridge; this, like the sun,
Extracts the dew from my declining soul   55
And swims mine eyes in moist effeminacy.
Oh Bess, Bess, Bess, Bess.

JOFFER.

Dead pity you have wakened in my bosom
And made me with you like compassionate.
Freely relate your sorrows.

SPENCER.   Sir, I shall.   60
If you have ever loved or such a maid
So fair, so constant, and so chaste as mine,
And should fortune, too lamentable fortune,
Betray her to a black, abortive fate,
How would it wring you? Or if you had a heart   65
Made of that metal that we white men have,
How would it melt in you?

JOFFER.   Sir, you confound me.

SPENCER.

I will be brief. The travels of my Bess

50. at] *Shepherd*; an *Q*.

---

46. *misprize*] mistake, underestimate.

49. *stakes . . . wheel*] Possibly *stakes* should be singular (meaning the stake
to which one was bound for burning), but criminals were sometimes impaled
and presumably more than one stake could be employed for this purpose. By
pikes Spencer probably refers to "passing the pikes," running the gauntlet.
The *cauldron* contained some such uncomfortable substance as hot oil or
molten lead, and one was tied to a *wheel* to be tortured in various ways,
usually by having his bones broken.

61. *or*] ere, any at all.

66. *metal*] still the same word as "mettle" (disposition); here "mettle" is
meant, but "metal" is required by the metaphor.

To find me out, you have partook at full
In presence of the king; these I omit.   70
Now when we came to sum up all our joy
And this night were ent'ring to our hoped bliss,
The king (oh, most unworthy of that name!)
He quite fell off from goodness.

JOFFER.   Who, Mullisheg?

SPENCER.

His lust outweigh'd his honor, and as if his soul   75
Were blacker than his face, he laid plots
To take this sweet night from me; but prevented,
I have convey'd my beauteous bride aboard.
My captain and lieutenant—

JOFFER.   Are they escap'd?

SPENCER.

Safe to my *Negro*. Thus far fortune led me   80
Through many dangers till I pass'd this bridge,
The last of all your watches. And muse not,
Bashaw, that I thus single durst oppose myself.
I wore my mistress here, and she, not I,
Made me midway a conqueror.

JOFFER.   She being at sea   85
And safe, why should your own fates trouble you?

SPENCER.

Renowned Moor, there is your greatest error.
When we parted, I swore by the honor of a gentleman
And as I ever was her constant friend,
If I surviv'd to visit her aboard   90
By such an hour; but if I fail, that she
Should think me dead. Now if I break one minute,
She leaps into the sea. 'Tis this, great Bashaw,
That from a soldier's eyes draws pearly tears.
For my own person, I despise all fears.   95

JOFFER.

You have deeply touch'd me, and to let you know

---

77. *prevented*] provided beforehand (i.e., forewarned).

85. *Made . . . conqueror*] enabled me to overcome half the obstacles in my way.

92. *break*] fail to keep my promise by.

All moral virtues are not solely grounded
In th' hearts of Christians, go and pass free.
Keep your appointed hour; preserve her life.
I will conduct you past all danger, but withal   100
Remember my head's left to answer it.

SPENCER.

Is honor fled from Christians unto Moors,
That I may say in Barbary I found
This rare black swan?

JOFFER.   And when you are at sea,
The wind no question may blow fair; your anchors,   105
They are soon weigh'd, and you have sea room free
To pass unto your country. 'Tis but my life,
And I shall think it nobly spent to save you,
Her, and your train from many sad disasters.

SPENCER.

Sir, I thank you.   110
Appoint me a fix'd hour. If I return not,
May I be held a scorn to Christendom
And recreant to my country.

JOFFER.

By three tomorrow.

SPENCER.   Bind me by some oath.

JOFFER.

Only your hand and word.

SPENCER.   Which if I break—   115
What my heart thinks, my tongue forbears to speak.

JOFFER.

I'll bear you past all watches.   *Exeunt.*

Explicit Actus secundus.

[III.i]   *Enter* Mullisheg.

MULLISHEG.

Through satiate with the pleasures of this night,

---

104. *black swan*] The swan generally was an emblem of excellence; the
black swan was proverbially of extreme rarity.
[III.i]
   1. *Through*] thoroughly.

The morning calls me from the sweet embraces
Of the fair English damsel.

[Enter Tota, *unseen by* Mullisheg.]

TOTA.   The English stranger
Is stol'n from forth mine arms. I am at full revenged.
Were I again to match, I'd marry one   5
Of this brave nation, if a gentleman,
Before the greatest monarch of the world,
They are such sweet and loving bedfellows.
Now to my chamber; darkness guide my way,
Lest what none yet suspect the night betray.   10
Let all like me wrong'd in their nuptial bed,
Not aim at th' heart, but rather strike at th' head.   *[Exit.]*

MULLISHEG.

Venetian ladies, nor the Persian girls,
The French, the Spanish, nor the Turkish dames,
Ethiope, nor Greece can kiss with half that art   15
These English can, nor entertain their friends
Wi' th' tenth part of that ample willingness
Within their arms.

Enter [Bashaw Alcade].

ALCADE.

Your highness call'd?

MULLISHEG.

To tell thee that none shall partake but thou.   20
Oh, I have had the sweetest night's content
That ever king enjoy'd.

ALCADE.   With the fair English bride.

MULLISHEG.

Nor envy if I raise the captain for't,
For he shall mount.

ALCADE.

And he deserves it, but to me you owe   25
Part of that honor; I had a hand in't too,
Although perhaps you thought me ignorant
In what is past.

MULLISHEG.   Hadst thou no more

---

12. *th' head*] where the horns of the cuckold grow.

   Than half a finger in this night's content,
   It shall not be forgot, but thou as he   30
   Shalt be rais'd one step higher.

ALCADE.

   Observing what had pass'd, I spied the bridegroom,
   As still mine eyes were fix'd on him, up and late;
   Then by a trick,
   A pretty sleight, a fine fetch of mine own,   35
   I pass'd him forth the gates and gave command
   He should not have his entrance back again,
   Neither for reward nor entreaties, till day broke.

MULLISHEG.

   Your aim in that?

ALCADE.

   For fear lest he by some suspicious jealousy   40
   Should have disturb'd your rest.

MULLISHEG.   Thy providence
   Shall not die unrewarded. Shift him hence
   And with his will too!
   This makes thee of our council.

ALCADE.   'Tis an honor
   My wisdom hath long aim'd at, and I hope   45
   Now shall receive his merit.

Enter a Negro.

NEGRO.

   Pardon, great King, that I thus rudely press
   Into your private bedchamber.

MULLISHEG.   Speak, thy news.

NEGRO.

   The English captain, with the lovely bride,
   With her lieutenant, hath secretly this night   50
   With your highness' signet and the word
   Pass'd the court gates, pass'd all the watches, and
   Got aboard their *Negro,*
   And I was sent to know your highness' pleasure.

MULLISHEG.

   Ha, this night? —Alcade, seek, search;   55

35. *fetch*] stratagem.

I left her sleeping in our royal bed.

ALCADE.

I shall, my lord. —[*Aside.*]   I half suspect.   [*Exit.*]

MULLISHEG.

But was not Spencer with them?

NEGRO.   Only they three;

And we, by virtue of your highness' signet,

Pass'd them the court gates without trouble.   60

Enter Alcade.

MULLISHEG.

We are amazed. Alcade, whom find'st thou there?

ALCADE.

Nothing, my lord, but empty sheets,

A bed new toss'd, but neither English lady

Nor any lady else.

MULLISHEG.   We stand astonish'd,

Not knowing what to answer.   65

Enter a second Messenger.

MESSENGER.

Pardon, great King, if I relate the news

That will offend you highly.

MULLISHEG.

That the English captain, lady, and lieutenant are escap'd?

MESSENGER.

But that's not all.

MULLISHEG.   Can there be worse behind?

MESSENGER.

Yes, if the loss of your dear subjects' lives   70

Be worse than their escape. Spencer, without

The signet or the word, being left behind—

MULLISHEG [*to* Alcade].

You call'd the porter up, and let him after.

ALCADE.

Pardon, great King.

MULLISHEG.

Was this your trick, your sleight, your stratagem?   75

As we are King of Fez, thy life shall pay

The forfeit; thine own tongue shall sentence thee.—

But to the rest.

MESSENGER.   Then pass'd he to the bridge,
  Where stood armed men, in number forty.
  Maugre all their strength, with his good sword   80
  He would have made through all,
  And in this fierce conflict six, to the 'maze
  Of all the rest, were slain. Nor would he yield,
  Till suddenly we rais'd a loud alarm,
  At which the captain of the watch came down   85
  And so there surpris'd him.
MULLISHEG.   Is he prisoner then?
MESSENGER.
  In custody of the great Bashaw Joffer,
  With whom we left him.
MULLISHEG.   Command our bashaw
  To bring him clogg'd in irons.   [*Exit* Messenger.]
                    These English pirates
  Have robb'd us of much treasure, and for that   90
  His traitorous life shall answer. —[*To* Alcade.] But for thee,
  Traitor, that hadst a hand in his escape,
  Thou shalt be sure to pay for't.
ALCADE.   Alas, my lord,
  What I did was merely ignorance.
MULLISHEG.   Nay, bribes,
  And I shall find it so. —Bear him to guard.   95
                  [*Exit* Negro *with* Alcade.]
  What dissolute strumpet did that trait'rous captain
  Send to our sheets? But all our injuries
  Upon that English prisoner we'll revenge.
  As we in state and fortune hope to rise,
  A never-heard-of death that traitor dies.   [*Exit.*] 100

[III.ii] *Enter* Captain [Goodlack], Bess, Roughman, Clem.

BESS.
  No news from Forset yet that waits for Spencer?
  The long boat's not return'd?
GOODLACK.
  Not yet.

---

86. *surpris'd*] captured.

BESS.

Clem! To the maintop, Clem, and give us notice
If thou seest any like them make from the shore;   5
The day is broke already.

CLEM.

With all my heart, so you will give me warning before the
gunner shoots lest I tumble down again and put my neck a
second time in danger.

BESS.

Prithee, begone; let's have no jesting now.   10

CLEM.

Then I'll to the maintop in earnest.   [*Exit.*]

GOODLACK.

How fares it with you, Bess?

BESS.

Like a heartless creature, a body without motion.
How can I choose, when I am come to sea
And left my heart ashore? What, no news yet?   15

GOODLACK.

None.

BESS.

I prithee, Roughman, step into my cabin,
And bring me here my hour glass.

ROUGHMAN.   That I shall.   [*Exit.*]

GOODLACK.

To what end would you use it?

BESS.

Shall I tell thee, Captain?   20
I would know how long I have to live;
That glass once turn'd, the sandy hour quite run,
I know my Spencer's dead and my life's done.

Enter Roughman *with the glass.*

ROUGHMAN.

Your glass.

BESS.

Gramercy, good Lieutenant.   25
'Tis better than a gaudy looking glass
To deck our faces in; that shows our pride,
But this our ends those glasses seek to hide.

Have you been all at prayers?

BOTH.

　We have.   30

BESS.

　I thank you, gentlemen.
　Never more need; and you would say as I do,
　Did you but know how near our ends some are.
　Dost thou not think, Captain, my Spencer's slain?

GOODLACK.

　Yet hope the best.   35

BESS.

　This is the hour he promis'd. Captain, look,
　For I have not the heart, and truly tell me
　How far 'tis spent.

GOODLACK.

　Some fifteen minutes.

BESS.

　Alas, no more? I prithee tak't away;   40
　Even just so many have I left to pray
　And then to break my heartstrings. None that loves me
　Speak one word to me of him or any thing.
　If in your secret cabins you'll bestow
　Of him and me some tears and hearty prayers,   45
　We, if we live, shall thank you. Good gentlemen,
　Engage me so far to you.

Enter Clem.

CLEM.

　News, news, news!

BESS.

　Ha, good or bad?

CLEM.

　Excellent, most excellent; nay, super excellent. Forset and all   50
　his companions are rowing hither like madmen, and there is
　one that sits i'th' stern and does not row at all, and that is—
　let me see, who is it? I am sure 'tis he—noble Spencer.

39. S.P. GOODLACK.] *Collier; not in*
Q.

BESS.

    Spencer!
    Heart, let me keep thee; thou wast up to heaven   55
    Half way in rapture. —Art thou sure?

CLEM.

    I think you'll make a man swear his heart out.

BESS.

    Teach me but how
    I shall receive him when he comes aboard.
    How shall I bear me, Captain, that my joy   60
    Do not transcend my soul out of this earth,
    Into the air with passionate ecstasy?

Enter Spencer.

GOODLACK.

    Now, farewell Barbary. King Mullisheg,
    We have sea room and wind at will; not ten
    Of thy best galleys arm'd with Moors   65
    Can fetch us back.

ROUGHMAN.   For England, gentlemen!

BESS.

  Oh, where's the gunner?
  See all the ordnance be straight discharged
  For joy my Spencer lives; let's mist ourselves
  In a thick cloud of smoke and speak our joys   70
  Unto the highest heavens in fire and thunder.

ROUGHMAN.

    To make the queen vex and torment herself.

BESS.

    To make the king tear his contorted locks,
    Curl'd like the knots of furies. —Oh, this music   [*Shot.*]
    Doth please me better than th'effeminate strings   75
    Tun'd to their wild moriscos. Dance, my soul,
    And caper in my bosom, joyful heart,
    That I have here my Spencer.

GOODLACK.   Come, weigh anchor,
    Hoist sail. We have a fair and gentle gale
    To bear us to our country.

SPENCER.   Captain, stay.   80

BESS.

    I did not hear my Spencer speak till now,
    Nor would my sudden joy give me that judgment
    To spy that sadness in thee I now see.
    Good, what's the cause? Canst thou conceal't from me?
    What, from thy Bess? Whence came that sigh?   85
    You will not tell me. No, do not;
    I am not worthy to partake your thoughts.
    Do you repent you that you see us safe
    Embark'd for England to enjoy me there?
    Is there some other whom you better love?   90
    Let me but know her, and for your sweet sake
    I'll serve her too. Come, I will know the cause.

SPENCER.

    Know all in one.
    Now I have seen you, I must leave you, Bess.

BESS.

    Leave me? Oh, fatal!   *[Offers to fall.]* 95

SPENCER.

    Speak, my Bess; it is thy Spencer tells thee.

BESS.

    That he will leave me. If the same tongue
    That wounded me gives me no present cure,
    It will again entrance me.

SPENCER.   Arm yourself;
    It must be spoke again, for I must leave you.   100
    My honor, faith, and country are engag'd,
    The reputation of a Christian's pawn'd,
    And all that wear that sacred livery
    Shall in my breach be scandal'd. Moors will say
    We boast of faith, none does good works but they.   105

BESS.

    I am nor sleep nor waking, but my senses
    All in a confus'd slumber.

GOODLACK.   Sir, resolve us.
    You wrap us in a labyrinth of doubts,
    From which I pray unloose us.

SPENCER.   I shall.
    I made my way through slaughter, but at length   110

The watch came down and took me prisoner
Unto a noble bashaw. For my valor,
It pleas'd him to admire me; but when sorrow
To disappoint my Bess struck me in passion,
He urg'd me freely to relate my griefs,   115
Which took in him such deep impression
That, on my word and promise to return
By such an hour, he left himself in hostage
To give me my desires.

GOODLACK.   'Twas nobly done.
But what's the lives of twenty thousand Moors   120
To one that is a Christian?

ROUGHMAN.

We have liberty and free way to our country.
Shall not we take th'advantage that the heavens
Have lent us, but now, as if we scorn'd
Their gracious bounty, give up ourselves   125
To voluntary bondage?

BESS.

Prize you my love no better than to rate it
Beneath the friendship of a barbarous Moor?
Can you, to save him, leave me to my death?
Is this the just reward of all my travels?   130

SPENCER.

I prize my honor and a Christian's faith
Above what earth can yield. Shall Fez report
Unto our country's shame and to the scandal
Of our religion that a barbarous Moor
Can exceed us in nobleness? No, I'll die   135
A hundred thousand deaths first.

BESS.   Oh, my fate!
Was ever maid thus cross'd, that have so oft
Been brought to see my bliss and never taste it?
To meet my Spencer living after death,
To join with him in marriage, not enjoy him?   140
To have him here free from the barbarous Moors,
And now to lose him? Being so oft rais'd

---

113. *admire*] wonder at.
130. *travels*] carries as well the sense "travails."

-144-

Unto the height of all felicity,
To make my ruin greater? If you needs
Will hazard your own person, make me partner   145
In this thy present danger; take me with thee.

SPENCER.

Not for the world; no living soul shall bleed
One drop for me.

BESS.

Canst thou be so unkind? Then, false man, know
That thou hast taught me harshness. I without thee   150
Came to Mamorah, and to my country back
I will return without thee. I am here
In mine own vessel, mine own train about me.
And since thou wilt forsake me to embrace
The queen of Moors, though coining strange excuse,   155
E'en at thy pleasure be it; my way's into
My country. Farewell; I'll not shed one tear more.

SPENCER.

My parting's death,
But honor wakens me. The hour draws nigh,
And if I fail one minute, he must die.   160
The long boat now! —Farewell, Bess.   *Exit.*

BESS.   Why, farewell
Spencer; I always lov'd thee but too well.
Captain, thine ear.   [*Whispers to him.*]
This I have vow'd, and this you all shall swear.   *Exeunt.*

[III.iii]   *Enter* Mullisheg, Queen [Tota], Joffer, *Headsman.*

MULLISHEG.

Produce your prisoner, Bashaw.

JOFFER.   Mighty King,
Had you beheld his prowess and withal
But seen his passions, you would then like me
Have pitied his disasters.

MULLISHEG.

We know no pity for an injury   5
Of that high nature, more than our revenge.

151. Mamorah] *Collier; Momarah Q.*

We have vow'd his death, and he shall therefore die.
Go, bring him forth.

JOFFER.   Spare me, my lord, but some
Few hours, I shall.

MULLISHEG.   The least delay is death.

JOFFER.
    Then know, my lord, he was my prisoner.   10

MULLISHEG.
    How, was? And is not?

JOFFER.   By promise—

MULLISHEG.   Not in gyves?

JOFFER.
    He's gyv'd to me by faith, but else at liberty.

MULLISHEG.
    I pray unriddle us and teach us that
    Which we desire to know:
    Where is the English prisoner?

JOFFER.   I presum'd, my lord,   15
    Such noble valor could not be lodg'd alone
    Without some other virtues, faith and honor;
    Therefore, I gave him freedom to his ship
    Only upon his promise to return.
    Now if there be such nobleness in a Christian,   20
    Which, being a Moor, I have express'd to him,
    He will not see me perish.

MULLISHEG.   Foolish Bashaw,
    To jest away thy head. You are all conspirators
    Against our person, and you all shall die.
    Why, canst thou think a stranger so remote   25
    Both in country and religion, being embark'd
    At sea and under sail, free from our bands,
    In the arms of his fair bride,
    His captain and his sailors all aboard,
    Sea room and wind at will, and will return   30
    To expose all these to voluntary dangers
    For a bare verbal promise?

JOFFER.   If he comes not,

---

11. *gyves*] leg-irons, fetters.
27. *bands*] bonds.

Be this mine honor, King: that though I bleed,
A Moor a Christian thus far did exceed.

MULLISHEG.

    The hour is past;   35
    The Christian hath broke faith. —Off with his head!

Enter Spencer.

SPENCER.

    Yet come at last.

MULLISHEG.   Is't possible?
    Can England, so far distant, harbor such
    Noble virtues?

JOFFER.   I beshrew you, sir.
    You come unto your death, and you have ta'en   40
    Much honor from me and engross'd it all
    To your own fame. 'Twould have lived longer by me
    Than any monument can last, to have lost
    My life for such a noble stranger,
    Whose virtue even in this last act appears.   45
    I wish this blood, which now are friendly tears.
    You are come unto your death.

SPENCER.   Why, 'twas my purpose,
    And by that death to make my honor shine.—
    Great Mullisheg, cherish this noble Moor,
    Whom all thy confines cannot parallel   50
    For virtue and true nobleness. Ere my ship
    Should with such black dishonor bear me safe
    Into my country by thy bashaw's death,
    I would have bent my ordnance 'gainst her keel,
    And sunk her in the harbor.

MULLISHEG.   Thou hast slain   55
    Six of our subjects.

JOFFER.   Oh, had you seen
    But with what eminent valor—

MULLISHEG.   Naught that's ill
    Can be well done. Then, Bashaw, speak no more;
    His life is merely forfeit, and he shall pay it.

---

41. *engross'd*] monopolized.
59. *merely*] completely.

SPENCER.

 I am proud, Fez, that I now owe thee nothing,   60
 But have in me ability to pay.
 If it be forfeit, take it; lay all on me.
 I'll pay the debt; then set the bashaw free.

MULLISHEG.

 Besides misprizing all our gracious favors,
 To violate our laws, infringe our peace,   65
 Disturb our watch by night, and now, perhaps
 Having robb'd us of much treasure, stol'n to sea.

SPENCER.

 In that thou art not royal, Mullisheg.
 Of all thy gold and jewels lately given us,
 There's not a doit embark'd,   70
 For, finding thee dishonorably unkind,
 Scorning thy gold, we left it all behind.

TOTA.

 If private men be lords of such brave spirits,
 How royal should their princes be!

MULLISHEG.   Englishman,
 There's but one way for thee to save thy life   75
 From imminent death.

SPENCER.   Well, propose it.

MULLISHEG.   Instantly
 Send to thy *Negro* and surrender up
 Thy captain and thy fair bride; otherwise,
 By all the holy rites of our great prophet,
 Thou shalt not live an hour.

SPENCER.   Alas, good King,   80
 I pity and despise thy tyranny.
 Not live an hour? And when my head is off,
 What canst thou do then? Call'st thou that revenge,
 To ease me of a thousand turbulent griefs
 And throw my soul in glory for my honor?   85
 Why, thou striv'st to make me happy. But for her,

86. happy. But for her,] *Collier*;
happy but for her; *Q*.

_____

 64. *misprizing*] scorning.
 70. *doit*] bit (or perhaps more specifically: a *doit* was a Dutch coin of small value).

Wert thou the king of all the kings on earth,
Couldst thou lay all their scepters, robes, and crowns
Here at my feet, and hadst power to instal me
Emperor of th' universal empery, 90
Rather than yield my basest ship boy up
To become thy slave, much less betray my bride
To thee and to thy brutish lust, know, King
Of Fez, I'd die a hundred thousand deaths first.

MULLISHEG.
I'll try your patience. —Off with his head! 95

Enter Bess, Goodlack, Roughman.

BESS.
Here's more work. Stay!

SPENCER.
What make you here?
You wrong me above injury.

BESS.   If you love blood,
That river spare and for him take a flood;
Be but so gracious as save him alone, 100
And, great King, see, I bring thee three for one.
Spare him, thou shalt have more:
The lives of all my train—what say'st thou to't?—
And with their lives, my ship and all to boot.

SPENCER.
I could be angry with you above measure. 105
In your four deaths I die, that had before
Tasted but one.

MULLISHEG.
Captain, art thou there? Howe'er these fare,
Thou shalt be sure to pay for't.

GOODLACK.   'Tis my least care.
What's done is mine, I here confess't; 110
Then seize my life in ransom of the rest.

TOTA [*apart to* Roughman].
Lieutenant, you are a base villain.
What groom betray'd you to our sheets?

ROUGHMAN.
Please keep your tongue; I did you no dishonor.

---

90. *th' universal empery*] the empire of the whole world.

TOTA.

    Whom did you bring to our free embraces?   115

ROUGHMAN.

    'Twas the king; conceal what's past.

TOTA.

    Howe'er my mind, then yet my body's chaste.

ROUGHMAN.

    Make use on't.

SPENCER.

    Dismiss, great King, these to their ship again;
    My life is solely forfeit. Take but that,   120
    I shall report thee merciful.

BESS.

    It were no justice, King, to forfeit his
    And to spare mine; I am as deep as he,
    Since what my Spencer did was all for me.

GOODLACK.

    Great King, if any faulted then 'twas I;   125
    I led them on and therefore first should die.

ROUGHMAN.

    I am as deep as any.

JOFFER.   Oh, had my head
    Excus'd all these, I had been nobly dead.

BESS.

    Why pause you, King? Is't by our noble virtues
    That you have lost the use of speech? Or can you think   130
    That, Spencer dead, you might inherit me?
    No, first with Roman Portia I'd eat fire,
    Or with Lucretia character thy lust
    'Twixt these two breasts. Stood I engag'd to death,
    I'd scorn for life to bend a servile knee,   135
    But 'tis for thee, my Spencer. [*Kneels.*] What was his fault?

---

    118. *Make use on't*] take it to heart.

    132–133. *Portia . . . Lucretia*] Both were types of high Roman virtue and
resolution. Portia committed suicide by swallowing burning coals upon
hearing that her husband, Brutus, had been killed at the Battle of Phillipi.
Lucrece stabbed herself after she was ravished by Sextus Tarquinius
"because she would not live a by-word to Rome, nor preserve a despoiled
body for [her] husband's embraces" (Heywood, *Gunaikeion* [1624], p. 126).

    133. *character*] write in characters.

'Twas but to save his own, rescue his dear bride
From adulterate sheets, and must he die for this?

MULLISHEG.

    Shall lust in me have chief predominance?
    And virtuous deeds, for which in Fez   140
    I have been long renown'd, be quite exil'd?
    Shall Christians have the honor
    To be sole heirs of goodness, and we Moors
    Barbarous and bloody? —Captain, resolve me,
    What common courtesan didst thou convey   145
    Into our royal bed?

TOTA.

    I can excuse him. Pardon me, great King;
    I, having private notice of your plots,
    Wrought him unto my purpose, and 'twas I
    Lodg'd in your arms that night.   150

MULLISHEG.

    These English are in all things honorable,
    Nor can we tax their ways in any thing
    Unless we blame their virtues. —English maid,   [*Raises* Bess.]
    We give thee once more back unto thy husband,
    Whom likewise freely we receive to grace;   155
    And, as amends for our pretended wrongs,
    With her we'll tender such an ample dower
    As shall renown our bounty. But we fear
    We cannot recompense the injurious loss
    Of your last night's expectations.

BESS.   'Tis full amends,   160
    Where but the least part of your grace extends.

MULLISHEG.

    Captain, we prize thy virtues to thy friends,
    Thy faith to us, and zeal unto our queen.—
    And, Bashaw, for thy nobleness to a gentleman
    Of such approved valor and renown,   165
    We here create thee Viceroy of Argiers
    And do esteem thee next our queen in grace.—
    Y' have quench'd in me all lust, by which shall grow
    Virtues which Fez and all the world shall know.

156. *pretended*] intended.

SPENCER.

> We shall report your bounties, and your royalties   170
> Shall fly through all the parts of Christendom.

BESS.

> Whilst Bess has gold, which is the meed of bays,
> She'll make our English poets tune thy praise.—
> And now, my Spencer, after all our troubles,
> Crosses, and threat'nings of the sea's rough brow,   175
> I ne'er could say thou wert mine own till now.

MULLISHEG.

> Call this your harbor and your haven of joy,
> For so we'll strive to make it, noble strangers;
> Those virtues you have taught us by your deeds,
> We futurely will strive to imitate.   180
> And for the wrongs done to the hop'd delights
> Of your last night's divorce, double the magazine
> With which our largess should have swell'd your ship.
> A golden girl th'art call'd, and, wench, be bold;
> Thy lading back shall be with pearl and gold.   *Exeunt.* 185

[III.iv]   *Enter* Chorus.

CHORUS.

> Imagine Bess and Spencer under sail.
> But the intelligence of their great wealth
> Being bruited 'mongst the merchants, comes to th'ears
> Of a French pirate, who with two ships well rigg'd
> Waylays them in their voyage. Long they fought,   5
> And many slain on both sides; but the Frenchmen,
> Proud of their hopeful conquest, boarding twice,
> Are twice blown up, which adds courage to the English,
> But to the Frenchmen fear. Just as they buckl'd,
> Spencer and Goodlack, with two proof targets arm'd,   10
> Into the French ship leap, and on the hatches
> There make a bloody slaughter. But at that instant

---

172. *meed of bays*] reward of poetry.
182. *magazine*] store, collection.
[III.iv]
7. *Proud of*] made valiant by.   9. *buckl'd*] grappled.
10. *proof targets*] impenetrable shields.

The billows swell'd, the winds grew high and loud,
And as the soul and body use to part,
With no less force these lovers are divided. *Come on!*   15
He wafts to her and she makes signs to him.
He calls and she replies. They both grow hoarse
With shrieking out their last farewell. Now she swoons
And sinks beneath the arms of Roughman. Spencer
Upon a chest gets hold and safe arrives   20
I'th' Marquis of Ferrara's country. The like adventure
Chanc'd Goodlack; upon a mast he pierces Italy,
Where these two dukes were then at odds. Spencer is chosen
Ferrara's champion; Mantua makes Goodlack his.
What happen'd them, if you desire to know,   25
To cut off words, we'll act it in dumb show.

Dumb Show.

The Dukes by them aton'd, they, graced and preferr'd,
Take their next way towards Florence. What of Bess,
Roughman, and Clem becomes, must next succeed.
The seas to them like cruel proves, and wrecks   30
Their *Negro* on the coast of Florence, where
They wander up and down 'mongst the banditties.
More of their fortunes we will next pursue,
In which we mean to be as brief as true.   *Exit.*

Explicit Actus tertius.

[IV.i]   *Enter* Bess, Roughman, *and* Clem.

BESS.

    All is lost.

ROUGHMAN.

    Save these ourselves.

CLEM.

    For my part, I have not so much left as a clean shirt.

---

  16. *wafts*] waves.
  19. *beneath*] down into.
  22. *pierces*] reaches, enters (cf. Pt. II, V.i.70).
  27. *preferr'd*] rewarded, given privileges.
[IV.i]
  2. *Save . . . ourselves*] except our very selves.

BESS.

> And Spencer too. Had the seas left me him,
> I should have thought them kind, but in his fate   5
> All wishes, fortunes, hopes of better days
> Expire.

ROUGHMAN.

> Spencer may live.

CLEM.

> Ay, that he may, if it be but in a sea-water green suit, as I
> was, among the haddocks.   10

BESS.

> How many bitter plunges have I pass'd
> Ere I could win my Spencer, who no sooner
> Married but quite divorc'd; possess'd for some few days,
> Then rent asunder; as soon a widow as I was a bride;
> This day the mistress of many thousands,   15
> And a beggar now, not worth the clothes I wear.

ROUGHMAN.

> At the lowest ebb
> The tides still flow; besides, being on the ground,
> Lower we cannot fall.

BESS.

> Yes, into the ground, the grave. Roughman,   20
> Would I were there; till then I never shall have
> True rest. I fain would know what greater misery
> Heaven can inflict, I have not yet endur'd.
> If there be such, I dare it; let it come.

> *Enter* Captain [of] Banditties, *and others.*

BANDIT.

> Seize and surprise the prisoners! —[*To* Bess.] Thou art
> mine.   25

25. Seize] *Collier*; Cease, Q (*see gloss*).

---

11. *plunges*] troubles.   12. *who*] i.e., to whom I was.
25. *Seize*] Q's *Cease* almost certainly means "seize," which could be so spelled, but the fact that it is followed by a comma in Q makes it just possible that the Bandit says "Cease!" (i.e., "Don't move!") to Bess and the others, and the rest of the sentence to his followers.

ROUGHMAN.

 Villain, hands off! Know'st thou whom thou offendest?

BANDIT.

 Bind her fast and after captive him.

ROUGHMAN.

  I will rather die
  Than suffer her sustain least injury.

        Roughman is beaten off. [*Exit* Clem.]

BESS.

  What's thy purpose?   30

BANDIT.

  In all my travels and my quest of blood,
  I ne'er encounter'd such a beauteous prize.
  Heavens, if I thought you would accept his thanks
  That trades in deeds of hell, I would acknowledge
  Myself in debt to you.

BESS.   What's thy intent,   35
  Bold villain, that thou mak'st this preparation?

BANDIT.

  I intend to ravish thee.

BESS.

  All goodness pardon me, and you, blest heavens,
  Whom I too boldly challeng'd for a misery
  Beyond my Spencer's loss. What, rape intended? 40
  I had not thought there had been such a mischief
  Devis'd for wretched woman. Ravish me?
  'Tis beyond shipwreck, poverty, or death.
  It is a word invented first in hell
  And by the devils first spew'd upon earth;   45
  Man could not have invented to have given
  Such letters sound.

BANDIT.   I trifle hours too long,
  And now to my black purpose. Envious day,
  Gaze with thy open eyes on this night's work,
  For thus the prologue to my lust begins.   50

BESS.

  Help! Murder! Rape! Murder!

BANDIT.

  I'll stop your mouth from bawling.

Enter Duke of Florence *and a train, and* Merchant.

FLORENCE.

    This way the cry came. —Rescue for the lady!—
    Hold thy desperate fury, and arm thyself
    For my encounter.

BANDIT.   Hell! Prevented!   *[Exit with followers.]*   55

FLORENCE.

    Unbind that beauteous lady and pursue
    The ruffin; he that can bring his head shall have
    A thousand crowns propos'd for his reward.
    He should be captain of those bloody thieves
    That haunts our mountains and of our dear subjects   60
    Hath oft made outrage. —Go, see this proclaim'd.
                         [Exeunt some of the train.]

BESS.

    Ere I the happy wishes of my soul,
    My orisons to heaven, or make free tender
    Of a most bounden duty, grace my misery
    To let me know unto what worthy person,   65
    Of what degree or state, I owe the service
    Of a most wretched life, lest in my ignorance
    I prove an heretic to all good manners
    And harshly so offend.   *[Kneels.]*

FLORENCE.

    Fairest of thy sex, I need not question thine,   70
    Because I read a nobleness in thy forehead;
    But, to resolve thee, know I am styl'd the Duke
    Of Florence and of this country prince.

BESS.

    Then from my knees I fall flat on my face
    In bound obeisance.   75

FLORENCE.

    Rise,   *[Raises her.]*
    That earth's too base for such pure lips to kiss.
    They should rather join with a prince's, as at first
    Made for such use. Nay, we will have it so.   *[Kisses her.]*

---

57. *ruffin*] devil.
62–64. *Ere . . . duty*] "Some mutilation here" (Dyce's notes).

MERCHANT [*aside*].

    That lady, if my memory be faithful   80

    Unto my judgment, I should have seen ere now,

    But where, what place, or in what country now

    I cannot call to mind.

FLORENCE.

    Where were you bred?

BESS.   In England, royal sir.

MERCHANT [*aside*].

    In England?

FLORENCE.   By what strange adventure, then,   85

    Happened you on these coasts?

BESS.   By shipwreck.

FLORENCE.

    Then churlish were the waves t'expose you to

    Such danger. Whence disembark'd you last?

BESS.   From Barbary.

FLORENCE.

    From Barbary? Our merchant, you came lately thence.

MERCHANT [*aside*].

    'Tis she; I now remember her.   90

    She did me a great courtesy, and I am proud

    Fortune, however enemy to her,

    Has given me opportunity to make

    A just requital.

FLORENCE.   What occasion,

    Fair lady, being of such state and beauty,   95

    Drew you from your own country to expose you

    To so long travel?

MERCHANT.   Mighty sovereign,

    Pardon my interruption if I make bold

    To put your grace in mind of an English virgin

    So highly grac'd by mighty Mullisheg.   100

FLORENCE.

    A legend worthy to be writ in gold,

    Whose strangeness seem'd at first to exceed belief;

    And had not thy approved honesty

    Commanded our attention, we should have doubted

    That thou therein hadst much hyperboliz'd.   105

---

105. *hyperboliz'd*] exaggerated.

MERCHANT.

    What would your grace give
    To see that miracle of constancy,
    She who reliev'd so many Christian captives,
    Redeem'd so many of the merchants' goods,
    Begg'd of the king so many forfeitures,   110
    Kept from the galleys some, and some from slaughter;
    She whom the King of Fez never denied,
    But she denied him love; whose chastity
    Conquer'd his lust and, maugre his incontinence,
    Made him admire her virtues?

FLORENCE.   The report   115

    Strikes us with wonder and amazement too;
    But to behold the creature were a project
    Worthy a theater of emperors,
    Nay, gods themselves, to be spectators.

MERCHANT.

    Behold that wonder. —Lady, know you me?   120

BESS.

    Not I, I can assure you, sir.

MERCHANT.   I'll give

    You instance then. I was that Florentine
    Who, being in Fez, for a strange outrage there,
    Six of my men were to the galleys doom'd;
    But at your intercession to the king,   125
    Freely releas'd, for which in this dejection
    I pray accept these thousand crowns to raise
    Your ruin'd fortunes.

BESS.   You are grateful, sir,

    Beyond my merit.

FLORENCE [aside].   I cannot blame great Fez

    To become enamor'd on so fair a creature.—   130
    You had a friend much grac'd by that same Moor,
    Whom, as our merchant told us, you were espous'd to
    In the court of Fez. Where's he?

BESS.

    I cannot speak it without tears.

---

123. *strange*] unfamiliar, unknown to me.

FLORENCE.

    Why, is he dead?

BESS.   I cannot say he lives.   135

FLORENCE.

    How were you sever'd?

BESS.   It asks a sad relation.

FLORENCE.

    We'll find a fitter time to hear't. But now,

    Augment your griefs no further. On what coast,

    Pray, were you shipwreck'd?

BESS.

    Upon these neighboring shores, where all the wealth   140

    I had from Barbary is perish'd in the sea.

    I that this morn commanded half a million

    Have nothing now but this good merchant's bounty.

FLORENCE.

    You are richer in our high favor than

    All the royalty Fez could have crown'd   145

    Your peerless beauty with; he gave you gold,

    But we your almost forfeit chastity.

BESS.

    A gift above the wealth of Barbary.

FLORENCE.

    Conduct this lady to the city straight,

    And bear this our signet to our treasurer;   150

    Command for her ten thousand crowns immediately.

    Next to our wardrobe, and what choice of habit

    Best likes her, 'tis her own.

    Only for all this grace, deign, beauteous lady,

    That I may call me servant.

BESS.   Pardon, sir;   155

    You are a prince, and I am here your vassal.

FLORENCE.

    Merchant,

    As you respect our favor, see this done.

155. me servant./ Pardon, sir] *this*   vant./ Pardon me, Sir *Q*.
edn. (*Collier's suggestion*); you ser-

152. *habit*] costume.

BESS [*aside*].

> What must my next fall be, I that this morning
> Was rich in wealth and servants and ere noon   160
> Commanded neither, and next doom'd to death,
> Not death alone, but death with infamy?
> But what's all this unto my Spencer's loss?

FLORENCE.

> You to the city; we'll pursue the chase.
> Madam, be comforted; we'll send or see you.   165
> All your fortunes are not extinct in shipwreck;
> The land affords you better, if you'll be sway'd by us.
> As first you find us, we'll be still the same.—
> Oft have I chas'd, ne'er found so fair a game.   *Exeunt.*

[IV.ii]   *Enter* Clem *solus.*

CLEM.

> Where are my bashaws now? Let me see, what shall I do?
> I have left my mistress; where shall I have my wages? She's
> pepper'd by this, but if the captain of the banditties had had
> but that grace and honor that I had when I was in Barbary,
> he would not have been so lusty. She 'scap'd drowning,   5
> which is the way of all fish, and by this is gone the way of all
> flesh. My lieutenant, he's sure cut to pieces among the
> banditties, and so had I been had not my baker's legs stepp'd
> a little aside. My noble captain and Spencer, they are either
> drowned i'th' tempest or murdered by the pirates, and none   10
> is left alive but I, Clem, poor Clem. But, poor Clem, how wilt
> thou do now? What trick have you to satisfy colon here in a
> strange country? It is not now with me as when Andrea liv'd.
> Now I bethink me, I have a trade, and that, they say, will
> stick by a man when his friends fail him. The city is hard by, 15
> and I'll see and I can be entertained to my old trade of
> drawing wine. If't be but an underskinker I care not; better

---

3. *pepper'd*] ruined.   3. *by this*] by this time.

8. *baker's legs*] see Pt. I, II.i.37 n.

12. *satisfy colon*] appease hunger (*OED*).

13. *when . . . liv'd*] see Pt. I, V.i.110 and n.

16. *entertained to*] received into.

17. *underskinker*] apprentice barkeep.

do so than like a prodigal feed upon husks and acorns.
  Well, if I chance to lead my life under some happy sign,
  To my countrymen still I'll fill the best wine.   *Exit.*   20

[IV.iii]   *Enter* Roughman, *bleeding.*

ROUGHMAN.

  Wounded but 'scap'd with life. But Bess's loss: that's it that
  grieves me inward. Ravish'd perhaps and murdered. Oh, if
  Spencer and Goodlack survive, how would they blame my
  cowardice! A thread spun may be untwined, but things in
  nature done, undone can never be. She's lost; they are   5
  perish'd. They are happy in their deaths, and I surviving left
  to the earth most miserable. No means to raise myself? I met
  a pursuivant even now proclaiming to the man could bring
  the head of the banditties' captain, for his reward a thousand
  crowns. If not for gain of gold, yet for he injur'd Bess, that   10
  shall be my next task. What though I die?
      Be this my comfort, that it chanc'd me well,
      To perish by his hand by whom she fell.   *Exit.*

[IV.iv]   *Enter* Duke of Florence, Merchant.

FLORENCE.

  Our merchant, have you done to th'English lady
  As we commanded? Did she take the gold?

MERCHANT.

  After many compliments, circumstances,
  Modest refusals, sometimes with repulse,
  I forc'd on her your bounty. Had you seen   5
  What a bewitching art she striv'd to use,
  Betwixt denial and disdain, contempt and thankfulness,
  You would have said that out of a mere scorn

---

  18. *like . . . acorns*] "And he would fain have filled his belly with the
husks that the swine did eat . . ." (Luke 15:16).
  19. *sign*] i.e., of the zodiac.
[IV.iii]
  8. *pursuivant*] herald.
[IV.iv]
  3. *compliments*] polite expressions.
  3. *circumstances*] formalities.

T'accept your gift, she express'd such gratitude
As would demand a double donative.   10

FLORENCE.

And it has done't; it shall be doubl'd straight,
Arising thence unto an infinite,
If she'll but grant us love. How for her habit?

MERCHANT.

With an enforc'd will, wilful constraint,
And a mere kind of glad necessity,   15
She put it on but to lament the death
Of her lost husband.

FLORENCE.   Why, is he lost?

MERCHANT.

By all conjectures never to be found.

FLORENCE.

The less her hope is to recover him,
The more our hopes remains to conquer her.   20
Bear her from us this jewel, and withal
Provide a banquet. Bid her leave all mourning;
This night in person we will visit her.

MERCHANT.

I shall.

FLORENCE.

Withal more gold.   25
And if thou canst by way of conference
Get from her how she stands affected towards us,
It shall not be the furthest way about
To thy preferment and our special favor.   [*Exit* Merchant.]

Enter a Messenger.

MESSENGER.

The two bold dukes of Mantua and Ferrara   30
After many bloody garboils have enter'd league,
And within these two days mean to visit Florence
To make your court a witness of their late
Concluded amity.

FLORENCE.   We'll receive them

---

10. *double donative*] gift of twice the value.
31. *garboils*] disturbances.

As princes that in this would honor us.   35
MESSENGER.

These letters will speak further.
FLORENCE.   Bear them straight
Unto our secretary, and withal give order
That all our court may shine in gold and pearl.

[*Exit* Messenger.]

They never could have come in a happier season
Than when the great and high magnificence   40
Without suspect we would have shown to her
Will be accounted honor done to them.
In fate's despite,
We will not lose the honor of this night.   *Exit.*

[IV.v]   *Enter* Spencer, Goodlack.

SPENCER.

Ferrara was exceeding bountiful.
GOODLACK.

So was the Duke of Mantua. Had we stay'd
Within their confines, we might even till death
Have liv'd in their high favor.
SPENCER.   Oh, but Captain,
What would their dukedoms gain me without Bess,   5
Or all the world t'enjoy it without her?
Each passage of content or pleasing fortune,
When I record she has no part in it,
Seems rather as an augmentation
Of a more great disease.
GOODLACK.   This be your comfort: 10
That by this she's best part of her way
For England, whither she is richly bound,
There, when she is most hopeless of this your safety,
With your survival to receive us gladly
With an abundant treasure.
SPENCER.   But for that   15

13. There, when] *this edn.*; then
where *Q*.

---

8. *record*] recall.

I had sunk ere this beneath the weight of war
And choos'd an obscure death before the glory
Of a renowned soldier. But we are now
As far as Florence onward of our way.
Were it best that we made tender of our service   20
To the Grand Duke?

GOODLACK.

'Tis the greatest benefits of all our travels
To see foreign courts and to discourse their fashions.
Let us by no means neglect that duty.

SPENCER.

Where were we best to lodge?   25

GOODLACK.

Hard by is a tavern. Let's first drink there,
And after make inquiry who's the best
Host for strangers.

SPENCER.   Come ho, where be these drawers?

Enter a Drawer.

DRAWER.

Gentlemen, I draw none myself, but I'll send some.   [*Exit.*]

Enter Clem *with wine.*

CLEM.

Welcome, gentlemen. —Score a quart!   30

SPENCER.

Ha?

GOODLACK.

How?

CLEM.

No, no, I am an ass, a very animal; it cannot be.

SPENCER.

Why dost thou bear the wine back? —The slave thinks belike
we have no money!   35

GOODLACK.

What, dost thou think us to be such cashier'd soldiers that

---

28. *Come . . . drawers*] Dyce's notes suggest "Come, ho! some wine!
where . . . ." Words may have been omitted, yet the Drawer's *some* (1. 29)
may mean "someone," it being taken for granted that the strangers would
call for wine.

we have no cash? —[*Aside.*]   Tush, it cannot be he.

SPENCER [*aside*].

How should he come here? —Set down the wine.

CLEM.

I will, I will, sir. —Score a quart of— [*Aside.*]   Tricks, mere
phantasms. Shall I draw wine to shadows? So I might run   40
o'th' score and find no substance to pay for it.

SPENCER [*to* Goodlack].

Left we not him a' shipboard on his voyage towards England
with my—

GOODLACK.

With Bess; true. —Sirrah, set down the wine.

CLEM [*aside*].

Some Italian mountebanks; upon my life, mere juggling.   45

GOODLACK.

Upon my life 'tis Clem.

CLEM.

Ca—Ca—Cap—Captain? Master Spencer?

SPENCER.

Clem?

CLEM.

I am Clem.

SPENCER.

And I am Spencer.   50

GOODLACK.

And I Goodlack but cannot think thee Clem.

CLEM.

Yes, I am Clem of Foy, the Bashaw of Barbary, who from a
courtier of Fez am turn'd a drawer in Florence. But let me
clear my eyes better. Now I know you to be the same whose
throats the pirates would have cut and have spoiled your   55
drinkings.

SPENCER.

Oh, tell us, and be brief in thy relation,
What happened you after the sudden tempest
Sever'd our ships? Or what's become of Bess?

GOODLACK.

Where did our *Negro* touch?   60

40–41. *run o'th'*] continue adding to, run up the.

CLEM.

I'll give you a touch, take it as you will. The *Negro* and all
that was in her was wreck'd on the coast of Florence; her and
all the wealth that was in her all drown'd i'th' bottom of the
sea.

SPENCER.

No matter for the riches; where's she, worth more than ship   65
or goods?

GOODLACK.

Where's Roughman? For thou, we see, art safe.

SPENCER.

Nay, speak; where's Bess? —How my heart quails within me!

CLEM.

She, Roughman, and I were all cast ashore safe, like so many
drowned rats, where we were no sooner landed but we were   70
set upon by the banditties, where she was bound to a tree,
and ready to be ravish'd by the captain of the outlaws.

SPENCER.

Oh, worse than shipwreck could be!

CLEM.

I saw Roughman half cut in pieces with rescuing her, but
whether the other half be alive or no I cannot tell. For my   75
one part, I made shift for one, my heels doing me better
service than my hands; and coming to the city, having no
other means to live by, got me to my old trade to draw wine,
where I have the best wine in Florence for you, gentlemen.

SPENCER.

Ravish'd.

GOODLACK.   And Roughman slain.

SPENCER.   Oh, hard news.   80

It frets all my blood and strikes me stiff
With horror and amazement.

GOODLACK.   It strikes me

Into a marble statue, for with such

74. saw] *this edn.* (*Dyce's notes*); see
Q.

---

61. *give . . . touch*] tell you something that will affect you.
76. *one part*] *One* is an obsolete, erroneous form of "own" (*OED*), used
here for the sake of the wordplay later in the line.

I have like sense and feeling.

SPENCER.   Tell me, Captain,
    Wilt thou give me leave at length to despair   85
    And kill myself? I will disclaim all further
    Friendship with thee if thou persuad'st me live.—
    Ravish'd!

GOODLACK.   Perhaps attempted but prevented.
    Will you before you know the utmost certainty
    Destroy yourself?

SPENCER.   What is this world? What's man?   90
    Are we created out of flint or iron
    That we are made to bear this?

GOODLACK.   Comfort, sir.

CLEM.

    Your only way is to drink wine if you be in grief, for that's
    the only way, the old proverb says, to comfort the heart.

GOODLACK.

    Hark where we lie; and I prithee, Clem, let's hear from thee.   95
    But now leave us.

CLEM.

    I will make bold inquire you out, and if you want money (as
    many travellers may) as long as I have either credit, wages,
    or any coin i'th' world, you shall not want, as I am a true
    eunuch.   *Exit* Clem. 100

Enter Florence *ushering* Bess, *train.*

GOODLACK.

    Let's stand aside and suffer these gallants pass,
    That with their state take a whole street before them.

FLORENCE.

    Our coach stay. We'll back some half hour hence;
    Only conduct this lady to her lodging.—
    Ha, started you, sweet? Whence fetch'd you that sigh?—   105
    Our train lead on;
    W' have other business now to think upon.

Exeunt. Bess *casts a jewel.*

93–94. *drink . . . heart*] "Drink after grief goes merrily down" (Tilley,
D 596).

GOODLACK.

    Sure this was some great lady.

SPENCER.

    But observ'd you not this jewel that she cast me?
    'Tis a rich one.

GOODLACK.   Believe me, worthy your wearing.   110

SPENCER.

    What might she be to whom I am thus bound?
    I'm here a stranger; never till this day
    Beheld I Florence nor acquaintance found,
    Especially of ladies.

GOODLACK.   By their train
    The man that did support her by the arm   115
    Was of some special note and she a lady
    Nobly descended. Why should she throw you this,
    Being a mere stranger?

SPENCER.   There's some mystery in't,
    If we could find the depth on't; sure there is.

GOODLACK.

    Perhaps some newly fall'n in love with you   120
    Now at first sight, and hurl'd that as a favor.

SPENCER.

    Yet neither of us
    Had or the wit or sense to inquire her name.
    I'll wear it openly and see if any
    Will challenge it—the way to know her best.   125

GOODLACK.

    And I would so.

SPENCER.

    I'll truce awhile with sorrow for my Bess
    Till I find th'event.

GOODLACK.   And at best leisure
    Tender our service to the duke,
    Whom fame reports to be a bounteous prince   130
    And liberal to all strangers.

SPENCER.   'Tis decreed.
    But howsoe'er his favors he impart,
    My Bess's loss will still sit near my heart.   *Exeunt.*

113. found] *Brereton*; friend *Q*.

---

128. *find th'event*] discover the outcome.   131. *decreed*] decided.

[IV.vi]

Flourish. Enter Florence, Mantua, Ferrara [*with* Merchant *and train*].

FLORENCE.

    This honor you have done me, worthy princes,

    In leaving of your courts to visit me,

    We reckon as a trophy of your loves,

    And shall remain a future monument

    Of a more firm and perfect amity.   5

MANTUA.

    To you, as to the greatest, most honor'd,

    And most esteemed prince of Italy,

    After a tedious opposition

    And much effuse of blood, this prince and I,

    Late reconcil'd, make a most happy tender   10

    Of our united league.

FERRARA.   Selecting you

    A royal witness of this union,

    Which to express we come to feast with you,

    To sport and revel, and in full largess

    To spread our royal bounty through your court.   15

FLORENCE.

    What neither letters nor ambassadors,

    Soliciting by factions or by friends,

    Heaven's hand hath done by your more calmer temper.

MANTUA.

    All resistals, quarrels, and ripping up of injuries

    Are smother'd in the ashes of our wrath,   20

    Whose fire is now extinct.

FERRARA.   Which whoso kindles,

    Let him be held a new Herostratus,

    Who was so hated throughout Ephesus

    They held it death to name him.

0.1. *Merchant*] Q does not provide for his entrance. Collier brings him on with Roughman at IV.vi.122.1, but because there is no reason for his being in Roughman's company, it seems better to consider him one of Florence's attendants.

19 *resistals*] resistances.

22. *Herostratus*] On the night of the birth of Alexander the Great, Herostratus set fire to the temple of Artemis at Ephesus, so that his name would never be forgotten. The Ephesians *held it death to name him*, which, of course, insured the accomplishment of his purpose.

FLORENCE.   Nobly spoke.
And now, confederate princes, you shall find   25
By our rich entertainment how w'esteem
Your friendship. —Speak, have we no ladies here
To entertain these princes?

                    Enter Bess.

MANTUA.
Methinks I spy one beauty in this place
Worth all the sights that I have seen before.   30
I think, survey the spacious world abroad,
You scarce can find her equal.
FERRARA.   Had not wonder
And deep amazement curb'd my speech in,
I had forestall'd this prince in approbation
Of her compareless beauty.
FLORENCE.   Taste her, princes.—   35
    [*Aside.*] This surfeits me and adds unto my love
That they should thus admire her.
MANTUA.   Beauteous lady,
It is not my least honor to be first
In this most wish'd solicit.   [*Kisses her.*]
BESS.   I stand a statue
And cannot move but by another's will   40
And as I am commanded.
FERRARA.
I should have wrestled for priority,
But that I hold it as a blessing to
Take off that kiss which he so late laid on.   [*Kisses her.*]
FLORENCE.
Now tell me, princes,   45
How do you like my judgment in the choice
Of a fair mistress?
MANTUA.   You shall choose for me.
FERRARA.
More happy in this beauty I account you
Than in your richest treasure.
FLORENCE.   Wer't not clouded o'er

---

35. *Taste*] kiss.
39. *solicit*] entreaty or solicitation.

With such a melancholy sadness, I'd   50
Not change it for the wealth of Italy.—
Sweet, cheer this brow, whereon no frown can sit
But it will ill become you.

BESS.   Sir, I bleed.

FLORENCE.
    Ha, bleed?
I would not have a sad and ominous fate   55
Hang o'er thee for a million.
Perhaps 'tis custom with you.

BESS.   I have observed
Even from my childhood never fell from hence
One crimson drop but either my greatest enemy
Or my dearest friend was near.

FLORENCE.   Why, we are here,   60
Fix'd to thy side, thy dearest friend on earth.
If that be all, fear nothing.

BESS.   Pardon, sir;
Both modesty and manners pleads for me,
And I must needs retire.

FLORENCE.   Our train attend her;
Let her have all observance. —By my royalty,   65
I would not have her taste the least disaster
For more than we can promise.   *Exit* [*Bess, attended*].

FERRARA.
    You have only showed us a rich jewel, sir,
And put it in a casket.

MANTUA.   Of what country,
Fortune, or birth doth she proclaim herself?   70
For by her garb and language we may guess
She was not bred in Florence.

FLORENCE.
    Seat you, princes; I'll tell you a strange project.

                                        [*They withdraw.*]

---

    53. *Sir, I bleed*] at the nose, presumably. Cf. *The Duchess of Malfi*, II.iii:
"My nose bleeds./ One that were superstitious would count/ This
ominous. . . ."
    57. *Perhaps . . . you*] i.e., perhaps you are given to bleeding in this way.
    71. *garb*] Heywood seems to forget that Bess is dressed in a habit from
Florence's wardrobe (Pt. II, IV.i.152–153 and IV.iv.13–17).
    73. *project*] something thrown out or put forth (i.e., a tale).

Enter Spencer *and* Goodlack.

SPENCER.

I have walk'd the streets, but find not any that
Will make challenge of this jewel. Captain, now   75
We'll try the court.

GOODLACK.   Beware of these Italians.
They are by nature jealous and revengeful,
Not sparing the most basest opportunity
That may procure your danger.

SPENCER.   Innocence
Is bold and cannot fear. But see, the duke;   80
We'll tender him the solemn'st reverence
Of travellers and strangers. —Peace, prosperity,
And all good fates attend your royalty.

GOODLACK.

Behold, w'are two poor English gentlemen,
Whom travel hath enforc'd through your dukedom   85
As next way to our country, prostrate you
Our lives and service. 'Tis not for reward
Or hope of gain we make this tender to you,
But our free loves.

FLORENCE.   That which so freely comes
How can we scorn? What are you, gentlemen?   90

MANTUA [*indicating* Goodlack].

I'll speak for this.

FERRARA [*indicating* Spencer].

And I for him.

MANTUA.   Well met, renowned Englishman,
Here in the court of Florence. —This was he,
Great Duke, whom fame hath for his valor blazon'd
Not only through Mantua but through   95
The spacious bounds of Italy, where 'twas shown.

FERRARA.

Hath fame been so injurious to thy merit

92. S.P. MANTUA.] *this edn.; not in Q.*

---

86. *next*] nearest.   86. *prostrate*] present submissively.

97. *thy*] "Their" seems more natural, but *thy* may mean Florence's,
whose duty as a prince it is to recognize and reward deserving men. If it has
not informed him who these men are, fame has injured his merit by im-
pairing his magnanimity.

That this great court is not already fill'd
With rumor of their matchless chivalry?

FLORENCE.

If these be they, as by their outward semblance   100
They promise not much less, fame hath been harbinger
To speak their praise beforehand. Noble gentlemen,
You have much grac'd our court. We thank you for't,
And, though no way according to your merits,
Yet will we strive to cherish such brave spirits.   105

SPENCER.

Th'acceptance of our smallest service, sir,
Is bounty above gold. W'are poor gentlemen
And, though we cannot, gladly would deserve.

GOODLACK.

'Tas pleas'd these princes to bestow on us
Too great a character and gild our praises   110
Far above our deserts.

FLORENCE.   That's but your modesty.
English gentlemen, let fame speak for you.

FERRARA.

Gentlemen of England, we pardon you all duty;
We accept you as our friends and our companions.
Such you are, and such we do esteem you.   115

SPENCER.

Mighty prince, such boldness wants excuse.

FLORENCE.

Come, we'll ha't so.—
[Aside.] Amazement! Can it be? Sure 'tis the self-same jewel
I gave the English lady; more I view it,
More it confirms my knowledge. Now is no time   120
To question it. —Once more, renowned Englishmen,
Welcome to us and to these princes.

Enter Roughman [*with* Bandit's *head*].

ROUGHMAN.

Can any man show me the great Duke of Florence?

MERCHANT.

Behold the prince.

ROUGHMAN.

Deign, thou, renowned duke, to cast thy eyes   125

Upon a poor dejected gentleman,
Whom fortune hath dejected even to nothing.
I have nor meat nor money; these rags are all my riches.
Only necessity compels me claim
A debt owing by you.   130

FLORENCE.

By us?
Let's know the sum and how the debt accrues.

ROUGHMAN.

You have proclaim'd to him could bring the head
Of the banditties' captain for his reward
A thousand crowns. Now, I being a gentleman,   135
A traveller, and in want, made this my way
To raise my ruin'd hope:
I singled him, fought with him hand to hand,
And from his bloody shoulders lopp'd this head.

FLORENCE.

Boldly and bravely done. Whate'er thou be,   140
Thou shalt receive it from our treasury.

ROUGHMAN.

You show yourself as fame reports you,
A bounteous prince and liberal to all strangers.

FLORENCE.

From what country do you claim your birth?

ROUGHMAN.

From England, royal sir.

FLORENCE.   These bold Englishmen,   145
I think, are all compos'd of spirit and fire;
The element of earth hath no part in them.

MANTUA.

If, as you say, from England, we retain
Some of your countrymen. Know you these gentlemen?

ROUGHMAN.

Let me no longer live in ecstasy;   150
This wonder will confound me. —Noble friends,

126–127. *dejected . . . dejected*] As Shepherd points out (p. 443), this
repetition is suspicious, but one can only guess at the correct reading.
   138. *singled*] singled out.
   147. *element of earth*] which would give rise to melancholic humors,
making them retiring and cold of spirit.
   148. *retain*] have as part of our retinue.   150. *ecstasy*] astonishment.

Bootless it were to ask you why, because
I find you here. —Illustrious Duke, you owe
Me nothing now; to show me these is reward
Beyond what you proclaim'd. The rest I pardon.   155
FLORENCE.
What these are we know,
And what thou art we need not question much:
That head, though mute, can speak it.—
Princes, once more receive our royal welcome.—
[*Aside.*] Oh, but the jewel! But of that at leisure;   160
Now we cannot stay. —Our train lead on.   *Flourish.*

Exeunt Dukes, [Merchant *and train. Manent* Englishmen.]
SPENCER.
Oh, that we three so happily should meet
And want the fourth.
ROUGHMAN.   I left her in the hands
Of rape and murder, whence, except some deity,
'Twas not in the power of man to rescue her.   165
However, a good office I have done her,
Which even in death her soul will thank me for,
Reveng'd her on that villain.
GOODLACK.
It hath express'd the nobleness of thy spirit;
For it we still shall owe thee.   170
ROUGHMAN.
But what adventure hath preferr'd you,
And brought you thus in grace?
GOODLACK.   You shall hereafter
Partake of that at large. But leaving this discourse,
With our joint persuasions let's strive
To comfort him, that's nothing but discomfort.   175
ROUGHMAN.
Would I had brought him news of that rare virtue!
Yet you have never heard of our late shipwreck.
GOODLACK.
Clem reported it.
ROUGHMAN.   How, Clem? Where's he?
GOODLACK.
He has got a service hard by and draws wine.

179. *hard by*] near by.

ROUGHMAN.

    His master may well trust him with his maids,   180
    For since the bashaws gelded him, he has learn'd
    To run exceeding nimbly.

Enter Merchant.

MERCHANT [*to* Spencer].

    Sir, 'tis to you, I take it, my message is directed.
    The duke would have some conference with you,
    But it must be in private.   185

SPENCER.

    I am his servant, still at his command.—
    Where shall's meet anon?

GOODLACK.   At Clem's.

SPENCER.   Content.

GOODLACK.

    Where we'll make a due relation
    Of all our desperate fortunes.

ROUGHMAN.   'Tis concluded.   *Exeunt.*

Explicit Actus quartus.

[V.i]   *Enter* Duke of Florence *and* Spencer.

FLORENCE [*aside*].

    I cannot rest till I am fully resolv'd
    About this jewel. —Sir, we sent to stay you
    And wean you some small season from your friends,
    And you above the rest because your presence
    Doth promise good discourse.

SPENCER.   Sir, I am all yours.   5

FLORENCE.

    How long hath been your sojourn here in Florence?

SPENCER.

    Two days; no more.

FLORENCE.   Have you since your arrival
    Retain'd no beauteous mistress? Pardon me,

---

    182. *run . . . nimbly*] not only because he is scared but also because he now
has no "stones" to weigh him down.

Sir, that I am come thus near you.

SPENCER.   On my soul,

Not any, royal sir.   10

FLORENCE.

Think it my love that I presume thus far

To question you. Have you observ'd no lady

Of special note, courted or discours'd with any

Within these two days?

SPENCER.   Upon my honor, none.

FLORENCE.

You are a soldier and a gentleman,   15

And should speak all truth.

SPENCER.

If otherwise I should disclaim my gentry.

FLORENCE.

I believe you, sir. You have a rich jewel here,

Worthy a prince's wearing. 'Twere not modesty

To ask how you came by it or from whom.   20

SPENCER.

Nor can I, sir, resolve you if you did;

But it was cast me by a lady, of whom

As then I took small notice of, my mind

Being troubled.

FLORENCE [aside].

'Tis even so.   25

SPENCER.

Perhaps your grace by knowing of this jewel

May know the beauteous flinger, and so you might

Engage me deeply to acquaint me with her

To prove her grateful debtor.

FLORENCE [aside].   No such thing.—

You know none in this city?

SPENCER.   Worse than scorn   30

Or foul disgrace befall me, if I know

Any you can call woman.

FLORENCE.   Be not moved;

---

9. *I . . . you*] I speak of such personal matters.

25. *'Tis . . . so*] i.e., just as I thought: he got the jewel from Bess.

29. *No . . . thing*] i.e., I certainly will not!

-177-

I spoke but this in sport. —[*Aside.*] Sure this strange lady,
Casting her eye upon this gentleman,
Grew straight of him enamour'd, which makes her   35
Keep off from my embraces; but I'll sound all,
Yet my own wrongs prevent. —Sir, I stay'd you
But to another purpose, to commit
A weighty secret to you.
SPENCER.   Wer't of millions,
I'd prove your faithful steward.   40
FLORENCE.
    I have a mistress that I tender dearer
    Than mine own eyes (observe me nearer, sir)
    Whom neither courtship moves, favors can work,
    Nor no preferment tempt.
SPENCER.   How rich were he
    Could call himself lord of such a jewel.   45
FLORENCE.
    My entreaties, friends, persuasions, importunities
    Of my chaste ladies cannot prevail at all.
    Now would I choose a stranger, selecting thee,
    To bear to her these few lines, which contain
    The substance of my mind.
SPENCER.   And, sir, I shall.   50
FLORENCE.
    In thy aspect
    I read a fortune that should destine me
    To strange felicities. Wilt thou be faithful?
SPENCER.
    As to my soul.
FLORENCE.
    But thou shalt swear before thou undertak'st it   55
    (Though I suspect not falsehood in thy visage)
    Not once to cast on her an amorous look,
    Speak to her no familiar syllable,

42. me nearer] *this edn.*; me, dearer
Q.

---

36. *sound*] fathom, understand.
42. *nearer*] Q's *dearer* seems to have been carried over from l. 41 through
some combination of misreading and memorial failure.

 Not to embrace her, nor to kiss her hand
 Nor her free lip by no means.
SPENCER.   Well, I swear.   60
FLORENCE.
 But that's not all.
 Swear by thy faith and thy religion
 Not to taste the least small favor for thyself,
 Touch or come near her bosom; for, fair stranger,
 I love her above measure and that love   65
 Makes me thus jealous.
SPENCER.   By my honesty,
 Faith, and religion, without free release
 From your own lips, all this will I perform.
FLORENCE.
 And so return the richest Englishman
 That ever pierc'd our dukedom. Instantly   70
 Thou shalt about thy task.   *Exeunt.*

[V.ii]   *Enter* Bess, Merchant.

BESS.
 You have tir'd our ears with your long discourse;
 Leave us to rest.
MERCHANT.   Dream on your best desires.
BESS.
 If at some half hour hence you visit us,
 We shall be free for language.
MERCHANT.   Soft rest with you. [*Exit.*]
BESS.
 If my soft sleeps presents me any shadow,   5
 Oh, let it be my Spencer's. Him whom waking
 I cannot see, I may in dreams perhaps
 Converse with. My sudden bleeding and my drowsiness
 Should not presage me good. Pray heaven the duke
 Prove loyal to mine honor. Howsoever,   10
 Death will end all, and I presume on this:

---

60. *free*] generous, open, inviting.
[V.ii]
 11. *presume on*] rely upon.

'Tis way to Spencer and my haven of bliss.   *She lies to sleep.*

Enter Spencer.

SPENCER.

What beauty should this be on whom the duke
Is grown so jealous? Sure 'tis some rare piece.
He told me she was fairer   15
Than I could either judge or yet imagine.
Would Bess were here to wager beauties with her,
For all my hopes in England. This is the chamber.
Ha, thus far off she seems to promise well.
I'll take a nearer and more free survey;   20
This taper shall assist me. Fail my eyes,
Or meet I nothing else but prodigies?
Oh, heavens, it is my Bess! Oh, sudden rapture!
Let me retire to more considerate thoughts.
What should I think but presently to wake her   25
And, being mine, to seize her where I find her?
Oh, but mine oath that I should never, never
Lie with her, being my wife, nor kiss her, touch her,
Speak to her one familiar syllable.
Can oaths bind thus? My honesty, faith, and religion   30
Are all engag'd; there's no dispense for them.
And yet in all this conflict to remember
How the duke prais'd her vertu, chastity,
And constancy, whom nothing could corrupt,
Adds to my joys. But on the neck of this,   35
It lays a double torture on my life,
First to forswear, then leave so fair a wife.   *She starts.*

BESS.

I am all distraction. In my sleep I saw him.
Could I but behold him waking, that were a heaven.

---

17. *wager*] contend in (as though for a wager).

18. *For . . . hopes*] despite what I hope for.

31. *dispense*] dispensation.

33. *vertu*] "vertue, goodness, honestie, sinceritie, integritie; worth, per-
fection, desert, merit; also valour, prowesse, manhood; also energie,
efficacie, force, power, might; also a good part or propertie, a commendable
qualitie" (Cotgrave, *A Dictionarie of the French and English Tongues* [1608]).

35. *on . . . of*] on top of.

Ha, do I dream still, or was I born to see   40
Nothing but strange illusions? Spencer! Love!

SPENCER.

    I am neither.

BESS.

    Thou hast his shape, his gait, his face, his language;
    Only these words of thine and strange behavior
    Never came from him. Let me embrace thee.

SPENCER.   No.   45

BESS.

    Then kiss me.

SPENCER.   No.

BESS.   Yet speak me fair.

SPENCER.   I cannot.

BESS.

    Look on me.

SPENCER.

    I must not, I will not; fare thee well.
    Yet first read that.

BESS.   I have read too much already
    Within thy change of looks.

SPENCER [aside].   Oh me, my oath;   50
    I'd chop off this right hand to cancel it.

BESS.

    But if not now, when then?

SPENCER.   Never.

BESS.   Not kiss me?

SPENCER.

    No.

BESS.   Not fold me in thine arms?

SPENCER.   No.

BESS.   Nor cast
    A gracious look upon thy Bess?

SPENCER.   I dare not.

BESS.

    Never?

SPENCER.   No, never.

BESS.   Oh, I shall die.   *She swoons.*   55

53. arms? No] *this edn.*; arms? Not *Q*.

– 181 –

SPENCER.

 She faints, and yet I dare not for my oath
 Once to support her; dies before mine eyes,
 And yet I must not call her back to life.
 Where is the duke? Some help! No ladies nigh?
 Are you all, all asleep or dead,   60
 There's no more noise in court?

    Enter Duke [of Florence] *and his train.*

FLORENCE.

 Ha, what's the business? Noble friend, what news?
 How speed you with my mistress?
SPENCER.   You may see:
 There on the ground, half in the grave already.
 So fare you well.—   65
 [*Aside.*] What grief mine is, those that love best can tell.
               [*Exit.*]

FLORENCE.

 Support her. —Speak, love; look up, divinest mistress.
BESS.

 You said you would not speak, nor look, nor touch your Bess.
FLORENCE.

 Who, I?
 By all my hopes, I ne'er had such a thought.   70
BESS.

 Oh, I mistook.
FLORENCE.

 Why do you look so ghastly about the room?
 Whom does your eyes inquire for?
BESS.

 Nothing; nay, nobody.
FLORENCE.   Why do you weep?
BESS [*aside*].

 Hath some new love possess'd him and excluded 75
 Me from his bosom? Can it be possible?
FLORENCE.

 All leave the chamber.   [*Exeunt train.*]
BESS [*aside*].

 But I'll be so reveng'd
 As never woman was. I'll be a precedent

To all wives hereafter how to pay home 80
Their proud, neglectful husbands. 'Tis in my way;
I've power and I'll do it.

FLORENCE.   What is't offends you?

BESS.
    'Tis you have done't.

FLORENCE.   We?

BESS.   If you be the prince.
    There's but one man I hate above all the world,
    And you have sent him to torment me here. 85

FLORENCE.
    What satisfaction shall I make thee for't?

BESS.
    This and this only. If you have any interest
    In him or power above him, if you be a prince
    In your own country, have command and rule
    In your own dominions, freely resign his person 90
    And his state solely to my disposure.

FLORENCE.
    But whence grows the ground of such inveterate hate?

BESS.
    All circumstance to omit,
    He and only he ravish'd me from my country.
    He was the cause of all my afflictions, 95
    Tempests, shipwreck, fears. I never had just cause
    Of care and grief but he was author of it.
    Speak; is he mine?

FLORENCE.
    What interest I can claim, either by oath
    Or promise, thou art commandress of. 100

BESS.
    Then I am yours;
    And tomorrow in the public view of all
    The stranger princes, courtiers, and ladies,
    I will express myself. This night I entreat
    I may repose myself in my own lodging 105
    For private meditations.

---

81. *in my way*] suited to my desires and capabilities.
103. *stranger*] foreign.

FLORENCE.   What we have promis'd
    Is in our purpose most irrevocable,
    And so, we hope, is yours.

BESS.

    You may presume, my lord.

                    [*Enter* Merchant.]

FLORENCE.

    Conduct this lady to her chamber;   110
    Let her have all observance. —We will lay
    Our strict command on him lest he should leave
    Our city before our summons. 'Tis tomorrow then
    Shall happy thee, make us most blest of men.   *Exit* Duke.

BESS.

    Now shall I 'quite him home. Th'ingrate shall know,   115
    'Tis above patience to be injur'd so.

MERCHANT.

    Will you walk, lady, or take your coach?

BESS.

    That we the streets more freely may survey,
    We'll walk along.   *Exeunt.*

[V.iii]   *Enter* Clem *with his pots.*

CLEM.

    Let me see—three quarts, two pottles, one gallon and a pint,
    one pint, two quarts more, then I have my load; thus are we
    that are under-journeymen put to't. Oh, the fortune of the
    seas! Never did any man that marries a whore so cast him-
    self away as I had been like i'th' last tempest; yet nothing   5
    vexes me so much that after all my travels no man that meets
    me but may say and say very truly I am now no better than
    a pot companion.

---

    115. *'quite*] requite.
[V.iii]
    3. *under-journeyman*] subordinate to a journeyman, apprentice (cf.
underskinker, IV.ii.17).
    5. *like*] likely to have, at the point of doing.
    8. *a pot companion*] (1) literally, a companion of pots; (2) a fellow-
drunkard.

Enter Bess, Merchant.

BESS.

That should be Clem, my man. —Give me some gold.—
Here, sirrah; drink this to the health of thy old mistress.—   10
Usher on;
We have more serious things to think upon.

[*Exeunt* Bess *and* Merchant.]

CLEM.

Mistress Bess! Mistress Elizabeth! 'Tis she. Ha, gold! Hence,
pewter pots; I'll be a pewter porter no longer. My mistress
turn'd gallant, and shall I do nothing but run upstairs and   15
downstairs with "Anon, anon, sir"? No, I have gold and
anon will be as gallant as the proudest of them. Shall I stand
at the bar to bar any man's casting that drinks hard? No,
I'll send these pots home by some porter or other, put myself
into a better habit, and say the case is alter'd. Then will I go   20
home to the Bush, where I drew wine, and buy out my time,
and take up my chamber, be served in pomp by my fellow
prentices.

I will presently thither,
Where I will flaunt it in my cap and my feather.   25

[*Withdraws.*]

Enter Goodlack, Spencer, Roughman.

GOODLACK.

You tell us of the strangest wonderment
That ever came within the compass of my knowledge.

SPENCER.

I tell you but what's true.

GOODLACK.

It cannot find example. Did you leave her
In those extremities of passion?   30

27. ever came] *possibly* ever'came   30. In] *Collier; not in* Q.
in Q.

---

18. *casting*] (1) reckoning (i.e., running up his bar account); (2) vomiting;
(3) shooting dice for drinks (?).
20. *the . . . alter'd*] things have changed (Tilley, C 111).
22. *take . . . chamber*] hire a room, as a regular patron would do.
30. *In*] Collier notes, "The preposition 'in' seems to have been accident-
ally battered out of the type, but a small part of the letter *i* is still visible." In

SPENCER.

    I think dying, or the next way to death.

GOODLACK.

    To cheer you,

    The duke's own witness of her constancy

    And virtue, arm'd against all temptations,

    Part of your griefs should lessen.

SPENCER.   Rather, friend,   35

    Augment my passions, to be forc'd to lose

    And quite abjure so sweet a bedfellow.

    Oh, it breeds more distraction.

GOODLACK.   Wer't my cause,

    I'd to the duke and claim her, beg for justice

    And through the populous court clamor my wrongs   40

    If he detain her from you.

SPENCER.   But my oath

    Ties me from that; I have quite abjur'd her.

    I have renounc'd her freely, cast her off,

    Disclaim'd her quite. I can no more

    Interest claim in her than Goodlack,   45

    Thou, or Roughman, thou.

GOODLACK.

    'Tis most strange. Let's examine all our brains

    How this may be avoided.

ROUGHMAN.

    How now, Clem; you loiter here. The house is full of guests,

    and you are extremely call'd for.   50

CLEM.

    You are deceived, my Lieutenant, I'll assure you.

    You speak to as good a man as thyself.—

    Do you want any money?

GOODLACK.   Canst thou lend me any?

---

52. thyself] *this edn.*; my self *Q*.

---

the copies of Q examined for this edition, something is visible after *her*, but
whether it is a fragment of an "i" is anybody's guess. As the type line ends
about two spaces short of the right margin, however, some small word was
doubtless there, and the context requires *in*. In Q the speech is printed as
prose, and *in* would not have been capitalized.

    48. *avoided*] voided, set at naught.

CLEM.

Look, I am the lord of these mines, of these Indies.

ROUGHMAN.

How camest thou by them?   55

CLEM.

A delicate, sweet lady, meeting me i'th' street, like an ass
groaning under my heavy burden, and being enamour'd of
my good parts, gave me this gold. If you think I lie, examine
all these pots, whose mouths, if they could speak, would say
as much in my behalf. But if you want any money, speak in   60
time, for if I once turn courtier again, I will scorn my poor
friends, look scurvily upon my acquaintance, borrow of all
men, be beholding to any man, and acknowledge no man;
and my motto shall be *Base is the man that pays.*

ROUGHMAN.

But, Clem, how camest thou by this gold?   65

CLEM.

News, news! Though not the lost sheep, yet the lost shrew is
found—my mistress, Mistress Elizabeth, 'tis she. She, meeting me i'th' street, seeing I had a pot or two too much, gave
me ten pounds in a purse to pay for it. *Ecce signum.*

Enter a Lord.

LORD.

The duke hath summon'd your appearance, gentlemen,   70
And lays his power of love, not of command,
To visit him in court.

CLEM.

I am put into the number, too. If he be a tall man, tell him
we will attend his highness.

LORD.

Fellow, my language was not aim'd at you.   75

---

66. *shrew*] literally, a shrew-mouse; however, "*sheep* and *shrew* are
contrasted as types of wives of opposite characters [as in] 'It is better to
marry a Shrew than a Sheep; for though silence be the dumb Orator of
beuty, ... yet a Phlegmatic dull Wife is fulsom and fastidious [i.e., un-
pleasant, disgusting]' " (1650; *OED*).
69. *Ecce signum*] behold the sign, look at the proof.
71. *lays*] asserts.
73. *tall*] worthy (Clem is playing the gallant).

CLEM.

But, sir, I'll make bold to come at first bidding.

LORD.

Sir, your reward stays for you at court
For bringing of the outlaw'd captain's head;
There's order ta'en for't from the treasury.

ROUGHMAN.

The duke is just and royal. We'll attend you.   80

CLEM.

And I'll go furnish myself with some better accoutrements,
and I'll be with you to bring presently.

[V.iv]   *Enter* Florence, Mantua, *and* Ferrara.

MANTUA.

There is not in your looks, renowned Florence,
That summer's calm and sweet alacrity
That was wont there to shine; a winter's storm
Sits threat'ning on your discontented brow.
May we desire the cause?

FLORENCE.   Which you shall know.   5
Princes, the fierce and bloody Moors have late
Committed outrage on our seas, especially
One mighty bashaw, 'gainst whom w' have sent
Petro Deventuro, one of our best sea captains;
And till we hear of his success, w' are barr'd   10
Of much content.

Enter Merchant.

MERCHANT.

My lord, good news. Petro Deventuro is return'd,
With happy victory and many noble prisoners,
And humbly lays his conquest at your feet.

Enter Petro, Bashaw [Joffer].

FLORENCE.

Petro, welcome.   15
This thy service shall not die unrewarded.
Freely relate the manner of thy sea fight.

---

82. *bring*] go (in company).

PETRO.

    Then thus, great Duke.
    This noble bashaw (noble I must call him,
    For he deserves that worthy attribute)   20
    Did lord o'er these our seas, appointed well,
    Laden with many a rich and golden spoil,
    Not weak to us in number; being in ken,
    We had him and his galleys straight in chase.
    He ne'er set sail or fled. Afar our ordnance play'd;   25
    Coming more near, our muskets and our small shot
    Like showers of hail begun the slaughter.
    There this bashaw, then perceiving straight
    That he must either yield or die, his scimitar
    He pointed to his breast, thinking thereon   30
    To perish, had not my coming stay'd him.

JOFFER.

    Nor think, bold Christian,
    That I can commend or thank thee for't,
    For who that's noble will not prize brave death
    Before a slavish bondage? Had I died   35
    By mine own hand, 't had been a soldier's pride.

FLORENCE.

    Although a prisoner captive and a Moor,
    Yet use him like the noblest of his nation.
    And now withdraw with him till we determine
    Of his ransom.   *Exit* [Petro *with* Joffer].   40

Enter Merchant *and* Bess; *also* Spencer, Roughman, Goodlack [*and* Clem].

MERCHANT.

    Way there for the duke's mistress!
SPENCER [*to* Goodlack].

    Ha, the duke's mistress, said he?
GOODLACK.   It was harsh.
BESS.

    Keep off. We would have no such rubs as these

---

    23. *in ken*] in sight.
    26. *small shot*] pellets smaller than musket bullets (like bird shot).
    43. *rubs*] obstacles (from the game of bowls).

Trouble our way, but have them swept aside,
A company of base companions,   45
To do no reverence to a prince's mistress!

SPENCER.

Hear you that?

MERCHANT.   Give back; you trouble the presence.

GOODLACK.

This cannot be Bess but some fury hath stol'n her shape.

[*They speak apart.*]

ROUGHMAN.

It seems strange.

SPENCER.   But unto me most horrid.

BESS.

Great Duke, I come to keep my promise with you,   50
If you keep your word with me.

FLORENCE.

These kind regreets are unto me more welcome
Than my late victory got at sea. Will't please you
Take your seat?

MERCHANT [*aside*].

Is not yon Spencer, and that the captain of the *Negro*?   55

SPENCER.

What shall we next behold?

FLORENCE.   Yet are you mine?

BESS.

From all the world, great Florence; witness this.— [*Kisses him.*]
You ne'er had yet a voluntary kiss.

SPENCER.

'Sfoot, I could tear my hair off.

FLORENCE.

Second your kindness. Let these princes see   60
Your tempting lips solely belongs to me.

BESS.

There's one again. It surfeits me 'bove measure
To be a prince's darling and choice treasure.

SPENCER.

Hold me, Goodlack, or I shall break out

52. *regreets*] greetings.
57. *witness this*] let this testify to it.

Into some dangerous outrage.

GOODLACK.   Show in this   65

Your wisdom, and quite suppress your fury.

FLORENCE.

Princes, I fear you have mistook yourselves

In these two strangers, for I have little hope

To find them worthy your great character.

MANTUA.

There must be great presumption that must force   70

Belief to that.

FERRARA.   Nay, more than presumptions, proofs,

Or they will win small credit.

FLORENCE.

You had from us, lady, a costly jewel;

It cost ten thousand crowns. Speak, can you show it?

BESS.

I kept it chary ·   75

As mine own heart because it came from you;

But hurrying through the street, some cheating fellow

Snatch'd it from my arm. Therefore, my suit is

With whomsoe'er the jewel may be found,

The slave may die.   80

FLORENCE.

His sentence thine; we never will revoke it.—

Our merchant, search all our courtiers and such

Strangers as are within our court.

MERCHANT.

Here's one of no mean luster, that this gentleman

Wears in his hat.   85

FLORENCE.

Reach it the lady.

GOODLACK.

This cannot be Bess Bridges, but some Medusa

Chang'd into her lively portraiture.

BESS.

Princes, the thief is found. Whate'er he be

That's guilty of this felony, I beg   90

---

87. *Medusa*] one of the Gorgons, slain by Perseus; she had snakes for hair
and her glance turned one to stone.

That I may be his sentencer.

FLORENCE.   Thou shalt.

BESS.

If you have any interest in his blood,
His oaths, or vows freely resign them, him,
And all at my dispose.

FLORENCE.   Have we not done't?

FERRARA.

Who can with the least honor speak for him,   95
The theft being so apparent?

CLEM [*aside*].

Now if she should challenge me with the purse she gave me
and hang me up for my labor, I should curse the time that
ever I was a courtier.

BESS.

Let me descend, and ere I judge the felon   100
Survey him first. 'Tis pity, for it seems
He hath an honest face. —[*To* Spencer.]   The word was
   "never."

GOODLACK.

What, Bess, forget yourself?

BESS.

An indifferent proper man, and take these courses?—
[*To* Spencer.]   You said you would not speak, nor look upon
   nor touch your Bess.   105

SPENCER [*aside*].

I could be a new Sinon and betray
A second Troy rather than suffer this.

BESS.

Good outward parts, but in a foreign clime
Shame your own country? —[*To* Spencer.]   Never think
   of that.

SPENCER [*aside*].

I fear my heart will break,   110
It doth so struggle for eruption forth.

FLORENCE.

When do you speak his sentence, lady?

---

106. *Sinon*] the Greek who induced the Trojans to bring the wooden horse
into Troy.

BESS.

You'll confirm 't whate'er it be?

FLORENCE.

As we are prince, we will.

BESS.   Set forth the prisoner.

MERCHANT.

Stand forward, Englishman.   115

BESS.

Then hear thy doom. I give thee back thy life,
And in thy arms throw a most constant wife.
If thou hast rashly sworn, thy oaths are free.
Th'art mine by gift; I give myself to thee.

FLORENCE.

Lady, we understand not this.   120

BESS.

Shall I make it plain? This is, great Duke, my husband,
Whose virtues even the barbarous Moors admir'd.
This the man for whom a thousand dangers
I've endur'd, of whom the best approved
Chroniclers might write a golden legend.   125

MERCHANT.

My lord, I know that gentleman
For Spencer and her husband, for mine eyes
Saw them espous'd in Fez. That gentleman,
As I take it, was captain of the *Negro*,
Th'other his lieutenant.   130

CLEM.

And do not you know me? Ha!

MERCHANT.

Not I, sir.

CLEM.

I am Bashaw of Barbary, by the same token I sold certain
precious stones to purchase the place.

FLORENCE.

Lady, you told us he was the author   135

---

125. *golden legend*] i.e., a narrative like *The Golden Legend* of Jacobus de
Voragine, a famous collection of saints' lives.
133. *by . . . token*] the proof being.
134. *precious stones*] i.e., those he parted with when castrated.

−193−

Of all your troubles, cares, and fears.

BESS.

I told true; his love was cause of all.
It drew me from my country in his quest
When I despair'd, and finding him in Fez—
Oh, do but think, great Duke, if e'er you lov'd,   140
What might have bought him from you. Had my Spencer
Been an Eurydice, I would have play'd
The Orpheus, and found him out in hell.

FLORENCE.

We now perceive
The cause of all these errors: his unkindness,   145
Grounded on his rash oath, which we release.
And all those virtues, honors, and renowns,
Which e'en the barbarous Moors seem'd to admire,
We'll dignify and raise their suffrage higher.

ALL.

Florence is honorable.   150

FLORENCE.

Bring in the bashaw. Call Venturo forth.

Enter Joffer, Venturo.

JOFFER.

Duke, I am prisoner; put me to ransom or to death. But to
death rather, for methinks a soldier should not outlive
bondage.

SPENCER.

Bashaw Joffer? —Leave my embraces, Bess,   155
For I of force am cast into his arms.—
My noble friend!

JOFFER.

I know you not; and I could wish you did not know me now
I am a prisoner, a wretch, a captive, and such a one as I

151.1. *Enter* . . . Venturo.]   *Collier*;
following l. 150 in Q.

142–143. *Eurydice . . . Orpheus*] Orpheus, a musician of marvellous skill,
charmed the infernal deities with his playing and nearly succeeded in
rescuing his wife Eurydice from Hades.

149. *suffrage*] opinion (i.e., we will honor him in such a way that his good
qualities will be better known).

would not have my friends to know. I pray, stand off.   160

SPENCER.

Because you are in durance, should I not know you? No,
For then the noblest minds should friends best know.
Have you forgot me, sir?

JOFFER.

No. Were I in freedom and my princely honors, I should
then be proud to call you Spencer and my friend. But now— 165

SPENCER.

An English virtue thou shalt try,
That for my life once didst not fear to die.—
Then for his noble office done to me,
Embrace him, Bess, dear Goodlack, and the rest,
Whilst to this prince I kneel. —This was the bashaw   170
King Mullisheg made great Viceroy of Argiers.
I know not, prince, how he is fall'n so low;
But if myself, my friends, and all my fortunes
May redeem him home, unto my naked skin
I'll sell myself. And if my wealth will not   175
Amount so much, I'll leave myself in hostage.

FERRARA.

'Tis the part of a most noble friend.

MERCHANT.

And in these times worthy admiration.

FLORENCE.

I wonder not the Moors so grac'd this nation,
If all the English equal their virtues.   180
For this brave stranger, so endear'd to thee,
Pass to thy country, ransomless and free.

ALL.

Royal in all things is the Duke of Florence.

JOFFER.

Such honor is not found in Barbary.
The virtue in these Christians hath converted me,   185
Which to the world I can no longer smother.
Accept me, then, a Christian and a brother.

168. Then] *Brereton*; That *Q*.   *notes*); made him great *Q*.
171. made great] *this edn. (Dyce's*

181. *For*] as for.

FLORENCE.

    Princes, these unexpected novelties
    Shall add unto the high solemnity
    Of your best welcome. —Worthy Englishman,   190
    And you, the mirror of your sex and nation,
    Fair English Elizabeth, as well for virtue
    As admired beauty, we'll give you cause
    Ere you depart our court to say great Fez
    Was either poor or else not bountiful.—   195
    Bashaw, we'll honor your conversion
    With all due rites. —But for you, beauteous lady,
    Thus much in your behalf we do proclaim:
        The fairest maid ne'er pattern'd in her life,
        So fair a virgin and so chaste a wife.   200

EPILOGUE

[Spoken at Court]

Still the more glorious that the creatures be,
They in their native goodness are more free
To things below them; so the sun we find
Unpartially to shine on all mankind,
Denying light to none. And you we may,
Great King, most justly call our light, our day,
Whose glorious course may never be quite run
Whilst earth hath sovereign or the heavens a sun.

FINIS

3. so] *Dialogues*; *as* Q. 8. heavens] *Dialogues*; *heaven* Q.
8. Whilst] *Dialogues*; *While* Q.

---

2. *free*] liberal.

Appendix A

The Cadiz Raid and the Islands' Voyage

Although the defeat of the Armada in 1588 ended any real Spanish threat to England, the Queen and her councillors, overestimating the strength of the Spanish navy and fearing another attack at any time, decided in the spring of 1596 to strike first by attacking the Spanish fleet based at Cadiz. As commanders in chief, Essex and the Lord Admiral, Charles Howard of Effingham, were instructed to destroy the Spanish ships and take their cargoes so that Spain could neither attack England nor aid the Irish rebels. This primary goal accomplished, the English commanders were then free to attack what Spanish towns they could. The English fleet sailed from Plymouth on June 1, arriving off Cadiz on June 20. Although the Spanish fleet was unable to put up much more than a nominal resistance, Essex and the Lord Admiral disregarded their instructions: in order to attack the nearly defenseless town, they allowed the enemy ships to escape, thus permitting the Spaniards to burn them rather than let them fall into English hands. By the evening of June 21, the English held Cadiz, and the next day they took the castle. Since ransom was not raised, the English burned the town and returned home, planning to make up for the riches they had lost through the destruction of the enemy ships by capturing the Spanish treasure-fleet as it left the Azores for Spain the following year.

Essex was given sole command of this expedition, the Islands' Voyage. With one hundred and twenty ships and a land army of six thousand he was to capture both the Spanish ships and the Azores, particularly the main island of Tercera. Essex left Plymouth June 3, 1597, but storms scattered his fleet, the ships finding haven where they could. He gathered his forces again at Plymouth, and after a month and a half of delay due to contrary winds and storms, the fleet again left Plymouth, arriving off the Azores on September 8. Hoping Tercera would fall more easily if the lesser islands were taken first, Essex planned a joint attack on Fayal with his subordinate Raleigh.

Raleigh reached the island first, and when, after several days, Essex had not yet appeared, he sent a small force ashore for fresh water. Heartened by the fact that the natives fled at their approach, Raleigh decided to take the town in spite of the fact that Essex was absent. The natives put up some resistance as the English approached the fort, but as the army advanced through the streets of the town, the people retreated, taking most of their valuables with them. The next morning September 22, Essex appeared, and Raleigh found himself accused of presumption in taking the town in his commander's absence. The English burned Fayal, but the Spanish fleet again escaped. Fearing the coming winter, Essex decided not to attack Tercera but to sail for home instead, picking up what Spanish ships he could find on the way. Essex left the Azores in mid-October. Storms again scattered his ships, and they arrived home separately. Although his forces were not able to take the Spanish *flota* on either expedition, Essex's exploits captured the imagination of the English people and won him much popularity.

Appendix B

The Actors of *The Fair Maid of the West*

[The following notes are based on information in Gerald Eades Bentley, *The Jacobean and Caroline Stage* (1941), Vols. I and II. As Professor Bentley points out (IV, 570), the failure of the dramatis personae of Part II to list the names of the actors for the five major roles no doubt indicates that these roles were taken in Part II by the same actors who played them in Part I. The only reassignment was of Anthony Turner, who played the kitchenmaid in Part I and Wilbraham's former role of the Bashaw Alcade in Part II.]

According to the Q title pages, *The Fair Maid* was acted by the Queen's Majesty's Comedians, or Queen Henrietta's Men. This company seems to have been formed in 1625, the coronation year, by Christopher Beeston, who had been associated with theatrical enterprises since about 1600 and who at this time not only had interests in the Red Bull, a popular public playhouse, but was also the owner and manager of the Cockpit Theater in Drury Lane, called the Phoenix since its conversion to a private theater in 1616. To make up the Queen's Men Beeston brought together a nucleus of experienced actors as well as some new personalities; their talents, combined with the favorable location of the Cockpit (near Whitehall), the services of the playwright James Shirley (who wrote exclusively or collaborated in twenty plays for their production), and Beeston's astute management (which included the maintenance of an excellent relationship with the court), established the troupe within a few years as one of London's most popular groups of actors, second only to the famous King's Men. The company lasted until 1636–1637, when Beeston brought a new group into being at the Cockpit; another Queen Henrietta's Men was later formed. Actor lists preserved in early editions of five plays and notations in the office-book of Sir Henry Herbert (a brother of George Herbert the poet, who carried out the duties of the Master of the Revels from 1623) show, as one would expect, some changes in the personnel of Queen Henrietta's Men during the life of the company, but at the time of the performance of *The Fair Maid* reflected in Q it included actors of considerable reputation. The four plays besides *The Fair Maid* which record roles taken by various members of the troupe are Massinger's *Renegado* (lic. 1624, pub. 1630), Davenport's *King John and Matilda* (written 1628–1634, pub. 1655), Shirley's *The Wedding* (written 1626–1629, pub. 1629), and Nabbes's *Hannibal and Scipio* (written 1635, pub. 1637).

ALLEN, WILLIAM (*Mullisheg*, Pts. I and II). A leading actor in the troupe during its time at the Cockpit, he had important roles in *The Renegado* and *Hannibal*. After Queen Henrietta's Men broke, he found a place with the King's company.

AXELL (Axall or Axen), ROBERT (*English Merchant*, Pt. I; *Duke of Mantua*, Pt. II). A secondary player who also appeared in *Hannibal* and perhaps in *King John* (where a Jackson, otherwise unknown, is listed).

BOURNE (Bird), THEOPHILUS (*Tota*, Pt. II). Probably the son of William Bird, an actor, Bourne for a time played women's parts, but had graduated to masculine roles by the time of *Hannibal*. He married Beeston's daughter, and was a successful actor after the Restoration.

BOWYER, MICHAEL (*Spencer*, Pts. I and II). Evidently an experienced actor, Bowyer played romantic leads for Queen Henrietta's Men. He later was a member of the King's company and was associated with the theater until his death in 1645.

CLARK, HUGH (*Bess Bridges*, Pts. I and II). He first appears as the female lead in *The Wedding*, a fact which suggests that his career probably began earlier. Like Bourne, he was soon to take masculine rather than feminine roles (he appears to have been married for several years at the time of his appearance in *The Fair Maid*), and in 1634 was one of the leaders of the company. He later was associated with the King's Men.

GOOD, CHRISTOPHER (*Forset* and *Spanish Captain*, Pt. I; *Duke of Ferrara* and *Forset*, Pt. II). A bit player with Queen Henrietta's Men, Good had more prominent parts in plays produced by the King's Revels company, which he later joined.

PERKINS, RICHARD (*Goodlack*, Pts. I and II). A friend of Heywood, Perkins was the most distinguished and probably the most experienced actor in the troupe. He was associated with the theater as early as 1602 and performed with several of the leading companies of the period, including the King's Men. Evidently he was quite versatile; his known roles include "romantic villain, dignified father, honest, plain-spoken old man" (Bentley, II, 526).

ROBINSON (Robbins), WILLIAM (*Clem*, Pts. I and II). Robinson played the clown part not only in *The Fair Maid* but also in *The Renegado*; one of his most famous roles was that of the Changeling. He evidently was with Queen Henrietta's Men during the lifetime of the company. He is said to have been shot by Parliamentary forces after their capture of Basing House in 1645.

SHEARLOCK (Sherlock), WILLIAM (*Roughman*, Pts. I and II). One of the leaders of the company, he took both comic and villainous parts, including doubled roles in *Hannibal*.

SOMNER (Sumner), JOHN (*Duke of Florence*, Pt. II). A regular member of the company, his specialty seems to have been dashing roles, like that of Florence and Mustapha, Basha of Aleppo, in *The Renegado*.

TURNER, ANTHONY (*Kitchenmaid*, Pt. I; *Bashaw Alcade*, Pt. II). A secondary member of the troupe, Turner took relatively inconspicuous roles most often (according to the surviving lists) those of old men.

WILBRAHAM, WILLIAM (*Bashaw Alcade*, Pt. I). Little is known of him. He appeared in *The Wedding*, and in March, 1634/35, he was performing in Norwich. In 1640 he appears to have loaned Beeston's widow £150 secured by a mortgage on the Cockpit.

Appendix C

Chronology

Approximate years are indicated by *, occurrences in doubt by (?).

Political and Literary Events	*Life and Works of Heywood*

1558
Accession of Queen Elizabeth I.
Robert Greene born.
Thomas Kyd born.

1560
George Chapman born.

1561
Francis Bacon born.

1564
Shakespeare born.
Christopher Marlowe born.

1572
Thomas Dekker born.*
John Donne born.
Massacre of St. Bartholomew's Day.

1573
Ben Jonson born.*

1574

> Thomas Heywood born, probably at Rothwell or Ashby-cum-Fenby, Lincolnshire.*

1576
The Theatre, the first permanent public theater in London, established by James Burbage.
John Marston born.

1577
The Curtain theater opened.

Holinshed's *Chronicles of England, Scotland and Ireland.*
Drake begins circumnavigation of the earth; completed 1580.

1578
John Lyly's *Euphues: The Anatomy of Wit.*

1579
John Fletcher born.
Sir Thomas North's translation of Plutarch's *Lives.*

1580
Thomas Middleton born.

1583
Philip Massinger born.

1584
Francis Beaumont born.*

1586
Death of Sir Philip Sidney.
John Ford born.

1587
The Rose theater opened by Henslowe.
Marlowe's *TAMBURLAINE*, Part I.*
Execution of Mary, Queen of Scots.
Drake raids Cadiz.

1588
Defeat of the Spanish Armada.
Marlowe's *TAMBURLAINE*, Part II.*

1589
Greene's *FRIAR BACON AND FRIAR BUNGAY.**
Marlowe's *THE JEW OF MALTA.**
Kyd's *THE SPANISH TRAGEDY.**

1590
Spenser's *Faerie Queene* (Books I–III) published.
Sidney's *Arcadia* published.
Shakespeare's *HENRY VI*, Parts I–III,* *TITUS ANDRONICUS.**

1591
Shakespeare's *RICHARD III.**

Admitted a pensioner of Emmanuel College, Cambridge (?).*

1592
Marlowe's *DOCTOR FAUSTUS** and *EDWARD II.**
Shakespeare's *TAMING OF THE SHREW** and *THE COMEDY OF ERRORS.**
Death of Greene.

1593
Shakespeare's *LOVE'S LABOR'S LOST;** *Venus and Adonis* published.
Death of Marlowe.
Theaters closed on account of plague.

Robert Heywood, a clergyman and probably the father of Thomas, dies. Thomas leaves Cambridge and goes to London (?).*

1594
Shakespeare's *TWO GENTLEMEN OF VERONA;** *The Rape of Lucrece* published.
Shakespeare's company becomes Lord Chamberlain's Men.
Death of Kyd.

Publication of the narrative poem *Oenone and Paris.*

1595
The Swan theater built.
Sidney's *Defense of Poesy* published.
Shakespeare's *ROMEO AND JULIET,** *A MIDSUMMER NIGHT'S DREAM,** *RICHARD II.*
Raleigh's first expedition to Guiana.

1596
Spenser's *Faerie Queene* (Books IV–VI) published.
Shakespeare's *MERCHANT OF VENICE,** *KING JOHN.**
James Shirley born.

Philip Henslowe records a loan to the Admiral's Men for "hawodes bocke."
Heywood under contract for two years to act only for Henslowe, probably with the Admiral's Men.

1597
Bacon's *Essays* (first edition).
Shakespeare's *HENRY IV*, Part I.*

1598
Demolition of The Theatre.

Shakespeare's *MUCH ADO ABOUT NOTHING,** *HENRY IV*, Part II.*
Jonson's *EVERY MAN IN HIS HUMOR* (first version).
Seven books of Chapman's translation of Homer's *Iliad* published.

1599

The Paul's Boys reopen their theater.
The Globe theater opened.
Shakespeare's *AS YOU LIKE IT,** *HENRY V, JULIUS CAESAR.**
Marston's *ANTONIO AND MELLIDA,** Parts I and II.
Dekker's *THE SHOEMAKERS' HOLIDAY.**
Death of Spenser.

JOAN AS GOOD AS MY LADY and *WAR WITHOUT BLOWS AND LOVE WITHOUT SUIT* (or *STRIFE*) written.
THE FOUR PRENTICES OF LONDON written.*

1600

Shakespeare's *TWELFTH NIGHT.**
The Fortune theater built by Alleyn.
The Children of the Chapel begin to play at the Blackfriars.

THE FAIR MAID OF THE WEST, Part I, written.*

1601

Shakespeare's *HAMLET,** *MERRY WIVES OF WINDSOR.**
Insurrection and execution of the Earl of Essex.
Jonson's *POETASTER.*

Becomes actor-sharer in the company of the Earl of Worcester.*

1602

Shakespeare's *TROILUS AND CRESSIDA.**

HOW A MAN MAY CHOOSE A GOOD WIFE FROM A BAD written* and published.
THE ROYAL KING AND THE LOYAL SUBJECT written.*

1603

Death of Queen Elizabeth I; accession of James VI of Scotland as James I.
Florio's translation of Montaigne's *Essays* published.
Shakespeare's *ALL'S WELL THAT ENDS WELL.**

Marries Ann Butler, June 13th(?).*
THE BLIND EATS MANY A FLY and *A WOMAN KILLED WITH KINDNESS* written.
Worcester's Men become Queen Anne's Men.

Marston's *THE MALCONTENT.**
Shakespeare's company becomes
the King's Men.

1604

Shakespeare's *MEASURE FOR MEASURE,** *OTHELLO.**
Marston's *THE FAWN.**
Chapman's *BUSSY D'AMBOIS.**

Performance before King James I of
HOW TO LEARN OF A WOMAN TO WOO.
IF YOU KNOW NOT ME YOU KNOW NOBODY, Part I, written.*

1605

Shakespeare's *KING LEAR.**
Marston's *THE DUTCH COURTESAN.**
Bacon's *Advancement of Learning*
published.
The Gunpowder Plot.

IF YOU KNOW NOT ME, Part I,
published. Part II written.

1606

Shakespeare's *MACBETH.**
Jonson's *VOLPONE.**
Tourneur's *REVENGER'S TRAGEDY.**
The Red Bull theater built.
Death of John Lyly.

IF YOU KNOW NOT ME, Part II,
published.

1607

Shakespeare's *ANTONY AND CLEOPATRA.**
Beaumont's *KNIGHT OF THE BURNING PESTLE.**
Settlement of Jamestown, Virginia.

THE RAPE OF LUCRECE written.*
A WOMAN KILLED WITH KINDNESS published.

1608

Shakespeare's *CORIOLANUS,** *TIMON OF ATHENS,** *PERICLES.**
Chapman's *CONSPIRACY AND TRAGEDY OF CHARLES, DUKE OF BYRON.**
Dekker's *Gull's Hornbook* published.
Richard Burbage leases Blackfriars
theater for King's company.
John Milton born.

THE RAPE OF LUCRECE published.
TROIA BRITANNICA entered in
Stationers' Register.

1609

Shakespeare's *CYMBELINE;**
Sonnets published.

FORTUNE BY LAND AND SEA
written (with Rowley).*

APPENDIX C

Jonson's *EPICOENE*.

1610

Jonson's *ALCHEMIST*.   *THE GOLDEN AGE* written.*
Chapman's *REVENGE OF BUSSY*
*D'AMBOIS.**
Richard Crashaw born.

1611

Authorized (King James) Version   *THE GOLDEN AGE* published.
of the Bible published.   *THE BRAZEN AGE* and *THE*
Shakespeare's *THE WINTER'S*   *SILVER AGE* written (perhaps
*TALE,** *THE TEMPEST.**   revisions of *HERCULES*, Parts I and
Beaumont and Fletcher's *A KING*   II, of *c.* 1595).*
AND NO KING.
Middleton's *A CHASTE MAID IN*
*CHEAPSIDE.**
Tourneur's *ATHEIST'S TRAG-*
*EDY.**
Chapman's translation of *Iliad*
completed.

1612

Webster's *THE WHITE DEVIL.**   *THE IRON AGE*, Parts I and II,
                                    written.*
                                    An Apology for Actors published.

1613

The Globe theater burned.   *THE BRAZEN AGE* and *THE*
Shakespeare's *HENRY VIII* (with   *SILVER AGE* published.
Fletcher).
Webster's *THE DUCHESS OF*
*MALFI.**
Sir Thomas Overbury murdered.

1614

The Globe theater rebuilt.
The Hope theater built.
Jonson's *BARTHOLOMEW FAIR*.

1615

                                    THE FOUR PRENTICES OF
                                    LONDON published.

1616

Publication of Folio edition of
Jonson's *Works*.
Chapman's *Whole Works of Homer*.
Death of Shakespeare.
Death of Beaumont.

1618
Outbreak of Thirty Years War.
Execution of Raleigh.
1620
Settlement of Plymouth, Massa-
chusetts.
1621
Middleton's *WOMEN BEWARE
WOMEN.**
Robert Burton's *Anatomy of Melan-
choly* published.
Andrew Marvell born.
1622
Middleton and Rowley's *THE
CHANGELING.**
Henry Vaughan born.
1623
Publication of Folio edition of
Shakespeare's *COMEDIES, HIS-
TORIES, AND TRAGEDIES.*
1624

THE CAPTIVES written for the
Lady Elizabeth's Men.
*Gunaikeion or Nine Books of Various
History Concerning Women* published.

1625
Death of King James I; accession of
Charles I.
Death of Fletcher.

THE ENGLISH TRAVELLER
written.*

1626
Death of Tourneur.
Death of Bacon.
1627
Death of Middleton.
1628
Ford's *THE LOVER'S MELAN-
CHOLY.*
Petition of Right.
Buckingham assassinated.
1630

THE FAIR MAID OF THE WEST,
Part II, written.*

1631
Shirley's *THE TRAITOR*.
Death of Donne.
John Dryden born.

THE FAIR MAID OF THE WEST,
Parts I and II, published.
Heywood begins to write civic
pageants.

1632
Massinger's *THE CITY MADAM*.*

THE IRON AGE, Parts I and II,
published.

1633
Donne's *Poems* published.
Death of George Herbert.

Marries Jane Span (?).
A MAIDENHEAD WELL LOST
written.*
THE ENGLISH TRAVELLER
published.

1634
Death of Chapman, Marston,
Webster.*
Publication of *THE TWO NOBLE
KINSMEN*, with title-page attribu-
tion to Shakespeare and Fletcher.
Milton's *Comus*.

LOVE'S MISTRESS written.
A MAIDENHEAD WELL LOST
published.
*THE LATE LANCASHIRE
WITCHES* written (with Brome)
and published.

1635
Sir Thomas Browne's *Religio Medici*.

The Hierarchy of the Blessed Angels
written.
Pleasant Dialogues and Dramas
written.*
A CHALLENGE FOR BEAUTY
written.*

1636

A CHALLENGE FOR BEAUTY
published.
LOVE'S MISTRESS published.

1637
Death of Jonson.

Pleasant Dialogues and Dramas pub-
lished.
*THE ROYAL KING AND THE
LOYAL SUBJECT* published.

1638

*THE WISE WOMAN OF HOGS-
DON* published.

1639
First Bishops' War.
Death of Carew.*

1640

Short Parliament.
Long Parliament impeaches Laud.
Death of Massinger, Burton.

LOVE'S MASTERPIECE written.*
*The Exemplary Lives . . . of Nine of
the Most Worthy Women of the World*
published.

1641

Irish rebel.

The Life of Merlin published.
Dies and is buried at St. James's,
Clerkenwell, London (?).

1642

Charles I leaves London; Civil War
breaks out.
Shirley's *COURT SECRET*.
All theaters closed by Act of
Parliament.

1643

Parliament swears to the Solemn
League and Covenant.

1645

Ordinance for New Model Army
enacted.

1646

End of First Civil War.

1647

Army occupies London.
Charles I forms alliance with Scots.
Publication of Folio edition of
Beaumont and Fletcher's *COM-
EDIES AND TRAGEDIES*.

1648

Second Civil War.

1649

Execution of Charles I.

1650

Jeremy Collier born.

1651

Hobbes' *Leviathan* published.

1652

First Dutch War began (ended
1654).
Thomas Otway born.

1653
Nathaniel Lee born.*

1656
D'Avenant's *THE SIEGE OF RHODES* performed at Rutland House.

1657
John Dennis born.

1658
Death of Oliver Cromwell.
D'Avenant's *THE CRUELTY OF THE SPANIARDS IN PERU* performed at the Cockpit.

1660
Restoration of Charles II.
Theatrical patents granted to Thomas Killigrew and Sir William D'Avenant, authorizing them to form, respectively, the King's and the Duke of York's Companies.

1661
Cowley's *THE CUTTER OF COLEMAN STREET*.
D'Avenant's *THE SIEGE OF RHODES* (expanded to two parts).

1662
Charter granted to the Royal Society.

1663
Dryden's *THE WILD GALLANT*.
Tuke's *THE ADVENTURES OF FIVE HOURS*.

1664
Sir John Vanbrugh born.
Dryden's *THE RIVAL LADIES*.
Dryden and Howard's *THE INDIAN QUEEN*.
Etherege's *THE COMICAL REVENGE*.

1665
Second Dutch War began (ended 1667).

Great Plague.
Dryden's *THE INDIAN EM-
PEROR.*
Orrery's *MUSTAPHA.*
1666
Fire of London.
Death of James Shirley.